A Bibliography of
Educational Administration
in the United Kingdom

D.A. Howell MA, PhD, DPA

NFER Publishing Company Ltd.

© N.F.E.R. 1978

Published by the NFER Publishing Company Ltd.,
Darville House, 2 Oxford Road East.
Windsor, Berks; SL4 1DF
Registered Office: The Mere, Upton Park, Slough, Berks. SL1 2DQ
ISBN 0 85633 151 1

Typeset by Jubal Multiwrite, 66 Loampit Vale, London SE13 7SN.
Printed in Great Britain by
Biddles of Guildford, Surrey.
Distributed in the USA by Humanities Press Inc.,
Atlantic Highlands, New Jersey 07716 USA.

Contents

Introduction

Educational administration as a field of study

The study of educational administration in the United Kingdom has developed largely along the lines indicated by Baron and Taylor,[1] with sociology of education, organizational analysis, role theory and management studies as the dominant influences on most recent work. Less account has been taken of the contribution which politically-based studies might make, whether in terms of administrative theory, decision-making, policy analysis, interest group theory or the like, although there are recent signs of some increasing interest in the politics of education. While there is in this country no such deep-rooted tendency to regard the fields of politics and education as being essentially discrete, and having nothing whatever to do with each other, which Harman found such a notable feature of the American and Australian scenes,[2] it remains true that on the whole students of government, public administration and politics have not really been interested over much in education and the education service. For their part, university education departments have not been particularly well equipped, at least until recently, to advance the study of educational administration; indeed in many quarters the study of educational administration has been conducted largely in an historical context. However the recent establishment of Chairs in related fields at Birmingham University and the Open University will, it is hoped, ensure that social and political studies play a fuller part in the development of this area.

As in other countries, the study of educational administration has always had the need of practitioners very much in mind. The need to develop courses of study, training and preparation for practising administrators and managers, which can be seen as relevant at least to their medium and long-term needs, has saved educational administration from the strictly-limited formal constitutional approach which has deservedly given some writing on public administration a bad name. What finds favour in many quarters at the moment, to judge by the content of *Educational Administration* (and its predecessor, the *Educational Administration Bulletin*) is a strong emphasis on applying management concepts and techniques to the study of educational institutions. There is some possible danger that the political and social aspects of educational administration may be overlooked in favour of the claim of educational management on the one hand, and public administration, or even public sector management, on the other. In this writer's view, such a narrowing of interest is much to be deplored.

Educational administration remains something of a special case. Many years ago, Roald Campbell,[3] writing with reference to North America, identified five main peculiarities in educational administration. These were the unique social function of education in society; the nature of the educational enterprise, being compulsory with usually no alternative available, and attended with considerable difficulties of evaluation; the character of the school administrator's major reference groups, and the nature of the publics with which he is confronted; the semi-professionalism of educational administration; and the dual role of the educational administrator, functioning both as an administrative officer of the local school board, and as an educational leader who needs to shape his organization to perform its tasks more effectively. Not all these considerations are applicable in equal measure to the current British scheme, yet there can be no doubt that the universality of the education service's clientele, the professional and managerial role of the administrator, and the nature of educational processes persist as factors which serve to mark off educational administration from related fields of study. In addition it embraces both the private and public sectors; universities and possibly other institutions of higher education cannot be described accurately as public organizations; nor does it make sense to describe or analyse their operations solely with reference to the criteria of public administration. An even more significant feature is the high degree of institutional autonomy within educational systems, which has no parallel whatever in other social services, and has considerable implications for the roles of both institutional managers and systems controllers. This autonomy now has to be considered in relation to yet another phenomenon marking off educational administration as a special case, namely the demand for a greater measure of lay accountability and responsiveness, which contains many ambiguities, and whose implications are not even now easy to describe. While educational administration obviously has many features in common with public administration, social administration and sociology, it cannot wholly be subsumed under any one of these, or even all of them in combination. It is a field of study best approached by a multi-disciplinary route, and it is in order to provide such a route that this Bibliography has been prepared.

The basis of the bibliography

The bibliography has been built up, in its essentials, from the teaching of educational administration as carried out or supervised by the University of London Institute of Education. This teaching takes place at several levels, ranging from options for the BEd degree and post-graduate Diploma in Education, via a specialist Diploma in Educational Administration for more senior practitioners, to higher degrees, based on taught courses and research. The teaching is multidisciplinary, its coverage broad and the approach eclectic and undogmatic. The theoretical approaches which have been developed include administrative theory and political science, in addition to those included in Baron and Taylor's survey. It is necessary to include in this bibliography a substantial amount of basic theoretical writing which has not been related directly to education, in view of the comparative lack of material which could justly be described as 'Theory of Educational Administration in the United

Kingdom'. The references collected here comprise only the more important British works. It would be out of the question, as well as distorting the general emphasis of this bibliography, to include a complete corpus of even one of these bodies of theory. Moreover, although in one sense theory is universal, its application is not, and even a universal-sounding theory may be grounded in studies of local circumstances. For these reasons, virtually no reference has been made to overseas writers. This may be thought harsh, especially on the Americans and the Australians, but again it would be far too easy to swamp the British material among the far more developed overseas work. It is worth emphasizing again that the study of educational administration consists of far more than a study of schools and colleges and their management. It also includes the study of educational systems and sub-systems and their components, as well as the relationship between the educational system itself and the wider political system, at both national and local levels. Moreover, educational administration is equally concerned with policies and processes as much as with institutions and systems. The bibliography starts, therefore, with separate sections on educational policy-making, and the government and control of the education system, and the identification of its main components. The most natural arrangement is to deal with the main components of the system first, namely governmental and other agencies, and to follow them with local education authorities, and then to list specific educational sectors. To some extent the available material dictates the arrangement, but some attempt has been made to produce a similar pattern throughout. It may be surprising at first sight how some areas seem very under-represented in relation to their importance, such as further education, and the voluntary and independent sectors. On the other hand, few people will be surprised at the much greater amount of material available on such areas as universities and the role of head teachers. The entries under 'Disputes' in the section devoted to local education authorities suggests that, contrary to the received wisdom, consensus does not always reign supreme.

A classification scheme which subordinated everything else

to the components of the system, sectors and institutions would give too narrow a view of educational administration. A separate section, therefore, has been devoted to the social aspects, so as to bring home that educational administrators operate in a social context, and are engaged in making provision to meet social needs, not simply to implement statutory provisions on a mechanistic basis, which might be efficient in a strictly limited sense (e.g. in the sense of providing roofs over heads), without being satisfactorily attuned to current social demands. Similarly it is necessary to give prominence to the control and management of the curriculum, and the deployment of educational resources, these being unique components of educational adminis-tration, and which would distinguish it, if nothing else did, from the inter-related fields of study mentioned earlier.

Educational systems and institutions are subject to the attentions of controllers of resources, providers of services, and articulators of demand. Separate consideration is clearly necessary for one main interest group, the teachers, as the principal providers of services, and this is by far the best documented. Other interests, whether controllers of re-sources (i.e. civil servants and elected members of local authorities), providers of services (chief education officers and their colleagues and other professionals) or articulators of demand (political parties, parental and other lay bodies) are mentioned separately under the appropriate section. It has been a recurrent and largely justified complaint of the Scots that the existence of their own very different edu-cational system has been largely ignored in recent com-mentaries, as well as in many, if not most, teaching programmes. It is hoped that the present collection of references to the Scottish system (and incidentally to those of the Welsh and of the Northern Irish) will do something to focus attention on the very significant differences to be found, and stimulate a more comparative approach to the study of educational systems in the UK.

The scope and coverage of the bibliography

Something must be said to explain how the boundaries have been drawn. There is deliberately no coverage of, or reference to, the economics or sociology of education, both of which are better developed disciplines in their own right, with their own corpus of reference material. Some overlap is inevitable, but this has been kept to a minimum. This overlap will be most apparent in the attention given to schools as organizations; and while some knowledge of financial planning and management is necessary to an understanding of educational administration, no attempt has been made to include references whose orientation is more obviously economic. So while the politics of financial control are included, the principles and techniques of manpower planning are not. However in view of the dearth of material in some areas specifically on educational administration, a few references have been collected, especially from local government or public administration which are clearly of general relevance even though their subject matter may not be. No attempt has been made to provide a picture of comparative educational administration (except within the United Kingdom) and almost no overseas material relating directly to the British educational scene has been included, with the exception of some OECD publications.

In preparing this bibliography, the primary aim has been to provide a guide to teachers and students of the subject, indicating the general state of the subject. It is also hoped that it will be of interest to practising administrators or managers who wish to know what has been written in fields of interest to them, and where it can be found. There is however a problem in deciding what kind of writings on the actual practice of educational administration should be included in a bibliography catering mainly for students and teachers of the subject. The decision has been taken to exclude much of this material as it would substantially alter the emphasis of the bibliography and admit a very large mass of highly diverse material, much of which deals with minute particulars. Such exclusion is an unfortunate necessity when one considers the importance of, for example, handbooks and pamphlets issued by educational organizations and interest groups on current issues and policies, guides to legislation and commentaries on new regulations and circulars, conference reports and manuals for administrators, if one seeks to understand how educational administration actually works. Similarly the educational press constantly produces material of great interest on almost every issue. But lines have to be drawn; and those interested in the detailed operations of educational authorities and institutions are referred to the final section of the bibliography as an initial source.

It is noticeable, and a matter for regret, how few practising administrators have contributed to writing on the education service. Perhaps they really are all too busy all the time. Consequently there is relatively little material available on the functioning of education departments as such; and some writing which is at first sight relevant to the needs of educational administrators (and students of educational administration) seems to go little beyond straightforward description, and contains virtually nothing on administrative aspects. Those hoping to learn about the administration of physical and professional resources in LEAs, or about the operation of institutions run by LEAs such as teachers' centres or outdoor pursuit centres, or about other aspects of the LEA administrator's work will have to search in the relevant sections, especially those devoted to LEAs and the management of schools and colleges.

It will be obvious that the material available is very unevenly spread, and that some fields have received much more sustained scholarly coverage than others. The net has therefore been cast fairly wide, so as to go beyond the usual range of professional journals. In addition to those periodicals which were scanned either thoroughly or selectively, many others, notably those listed in Section 11d, contain material which can be highly illuminating, and indeed indispensable for students of the educational scene. Much of the reporting in these other journals will be concerned with purely local issues, or with ephemeral matters; on the other hand, much will be good educational journalism, and many articles, notably in the *Times Educational Supplement* and the *Times Higher Education Supplement*, can certainly stand comparison with some of the journals selected for detailed scanning. Only one weekly has been scanned in detail, namely *New Society*. Nothing has been included which dates from before 1960, since educational administration had not really started then as a subject of academic inquiry, and in fact did not really get going for some time afterwards on any scale. In any event the bibliographies of Baron and Gosden[4] deal very fully with this earlier period. The bibliography is essentially of educational administration as a contemporary study, and to go further back in one's search for references would only over-emphasize the historical aspect, the strength of which is abundantly brought out anyway in most histories and surveys of the British educational system. The classification scheme is by design a fairly detailed one, so as to reduce the need for large-scale cross-referencing. It is hoped that readers will not find it difficult to trace what they want, even in a substantial area like the policy-making functions of DES, for example, by looking at the appropriate (or most nearly approximate) entries first under policy-making, then under the government and control of educational systems, and finally the educational sector concerned. There is bound to be some overlap of interest with other bibliographies, but their coverage of administrative issues is more specific. None, it appears, has the range of this one.

Finally, one may ask, looking at the material contained in this bibliography, in what fresh directions might the study of educational administration develop? There are some obvious major gaps, and on the other hand one or two areas which may possibly be reaching saturation point. For example, how many more studies of the role of the headmaster is there room for? This degree of coverage, however, is exceptional, and at the other extreme there is relatively little on the operation of the educational system as such, with comparatively little on LEAs and a remarkable scarcity of material on DES. Few educational policies have reached much sustained attention. There is, it is true, a clutch of case studies of secondary reorganization, but few of them are specifically related to each other, and there is still plenty of scope for a series of comparative case studies based on the same underlying theoretical approach. In contrast, much more attention has been given to the expansion of higher education, and notably universities. Perhaps a greater impetus for the study of educational systems could come, as Harman suggests,[5] from an application of Eastonian systems analysis, which could be instrumental in bringing back political science into the study of educational administration. There are too few writers in educational administration with a background in quantitative skills, and there is great scope here, not so much in the building of abstract models as for the development of quantitative techniques in educational planning and organizational analysis. The last great area awaiting exploitation is possibly that of examining how far one can study educational administration without acknowledging what is best described as the 'sociology of knowledge' approach. How far do practitioners and administrators operate, or think they operate, in a value free vacuum?

While it is true that probably most practitioners and many students would tend to play down the elements of conflict and emphasize the consensual aspects within educational administration, and would deny any conscious tendency to take decisions or to act on overt political grounds, how far can this apparent neutrality of attitude be sustained? On the other hand, is it forcing matters too far to interpret every decision and every proposal in terms of its effect on a value system which administrators are concerned either to defend or to attack? One of the old administrative proverbs is that educational administration all boils down either to personal relations or to common sense. The sterility and inadequacy of this does not need to be pointed out. However, is the opposite equally sterile in its own fashion, reducing all aspects of educational administration to the advancement or the repulse of a conscious or unconscious system of social control? To put it graphically, if perhaps a little unfairly, it was said of the critic Middleton Murry that he couldn't grill a sausage or clean his shoes without bringing God into it; is it impossible to have a significant discussion of e.g. examination schemes except in a context of social class relationships or the power structure?

Various acknowledgements should be made. Several of the bibliographies referred to have been consulted with profit, both in respect of their coverage and of their classification schemes. In particular, much has been gained from those of Baron, Blackstone and Harman. Thanks are due to the author's departmental colleagues for their general interest and for supplying copies of reading lists. Professor M.G. Hughes and Mr D.L. Parkes of the British Educational Administration Society gave a lot of initial encouragement, while special thanks must be given to Mr D.J. Foskett and his colleagues at the Institute of Education Library for their help at several stages. A particularly warm acknowledgment goes to Mrs Joan Ball and Mrs Caroline Bridges for their perform-ance of the demanding but tedious task of typing.

It may be that a revised edition of this bibliography will be called for in a few years' time; with this possibility in mind the author would be grateful for criticism (preferably constructive) and suggestions for improvement.

[1] Baron G. and Taylor W. (eds.) *Educational Administration and the Social Sciences* (1969).

[2] Harman, G.S. *The Politics of Education: a bibliographical guide* (1974), 3–4.

[3] Campbell, R.F. 'What makes educational administration a special case?' In: Halpin, A.W. (ed.) *Administrative Theory in Education* (1958).

[4] See items 809, 813.

[5] Harman, op. cit., 14–19.

Classification Scheme

b) schools as organizations

    i)   general   350—359
    ii) educational management   360—373
    iii) head teachers   374—395
    iv) teaching staff   396—405

c) pre-school provision   406—408
d) primary schools   409—414
e) secondary schools — general   415—429
f) comprehensive secondary schools   430—440
g) middle schools   441—443
h) VI form colleges   444—447
j) voluntary and private schools   448—453

6. *Institutional administration and management — higher and further education*   454—610

a) the further education system   454—466
b) FE institutions   467—482
c) higher education — general:

    i)   policy   483—495
    ii) administration   496—502

d) polytechnics   503—515
e) colleges of education:

    i)   policy   516—524
    ii) administration   525—532

f) universities:

    i)   government   533—543
    ii) Vice-Chancellors   544—547
    iii) administration   548—557
    iv) planning and finance   558—573
    v) research   574—576
    vi) student participation   577—590
    vii) new universities   591—597

10. *Scotland, Wales and N. Ireland* 765–800

    a) Scotland:

        i) Scottish Education Department annual
           reports   765–766
       ii) S.E.D. papers on teacher recruitment and
           supply   767–768
      iii) other S.E.D. papers   769–775
      iv) other Government papers   776–777
      v) other publications   778–790

    b) Wales   791–795
    c) Northern Ireland   796–800

11. *Information* 800–828

    a) Statistics:

        i)   official sources   801–805
       ii) other material   806–808

    b) bibliographies   809–820
    c) registers and guides to sources   821–826
    d) periodicals
    e) other material   827–828

Bibliography

Theoretical Approaches

1(a) *General*
1. BARON, G. and TAYLOR, W. (Eds) (1969). *Educational Administration and the Social Sciences*. Athlone Press.
2. BARON, G. *et al.* (1969). *Educational Administration: International Perspectives* Chicago: Rand McNally.
3. HOPPER, E. (ed.) (1971). *Readings in the Theory of Educational Systems*. Hutchinson.
4. HUGHES, M.G. (ed.) (1975). *Administering Education: International Challenge*. Athlone Press.

1(b) *Organization Theory*
5. ALBROW, M. (1970). *Bureaucracy*. Macmillan.
6. BROWN, R.G.S. (1965). 'Organization theory and civil service reform,' *Pub. Adm.* 46, 313.
7. BAILEY, P. (1972). 'The present need for organization and management studies in education,' *Br. J. Ed. Studs.*, XX, 148—53.
8. BENNETT, S.J. (1974). *The School: an Organizational Analysis*. Blackie.
9. BLAU, P.M. and SCOTT, W.R. (1963). *Formal Organizations*. Routledge and Kegan Paul.
10. GROSS, E. (1969). 'The definition of organizational goals,' *Br. J. Sociol.*, XX (3), 277—94.
11. GRAHAM, G. (1968). 'The theory of organizations, a note,' *Pub. Adm.*, 46, 191—202.

12. GRACE, G.R. (1972). *Role Conflict and the Teacher.* London: Routledge and Kegan Paul.
13. HOYLE, E. (1965). Organizational analysis in the field of education,' *Ed. Res.*, 7 (2), 97–114.
14. HARRISON, M. and others (1976). 'Barr Greenfield and organizational theory: a symposium,' *Ed. Adm.*, 5 (1), 1–13.
15. LIVINGSTONE, H. (1974). *The University, an Organizational Analysis.* Glasgow: Blackie.
16. MILHAM, S. and others (1972). 'Social control in organizations,' *Br. J. Sociol.*, XX, III (4), 406–21.
17. MORRISH, I. (1976). *Aspects of Organizational Change.* Allen and Unwin.
18. MOUZELIS, N. (1967). *Organization and Bureaucracy.* London: Routledge and Kegan Paul.
19. RICE, A.K. (1970). *The Modern University: a model organization.* Tavistock Press.
20. SILVERMAN, D. (1970). *The Theory of Organizations.* London: Heinemann.
21. SALAMAN, G. and THOMPSON, K. (1973). *People and Organizations* Longmans.
22. SHILS, E. (1961). 'The study of universities: the need for disciplined enquiry,' *Univs. Qu.*, 16, 14–19.
23. TURNER, C.M. (1977). 'An organizational analysis of the Further Education College,' *Voc. Asp. Ed.*, 24, 47–52.
24. TURNER, C.M. (1969). 'An organizational analysis of a secondary modern school,' *Sociol. Rev.*, 17 (1), 67–86.

1(c) *Politics*
25. DEARLOVE, J. (1973). *The Politics of Policy in Local Government.* Cambridge University Press.
26. HILL, D.M. (1974). *Democratic Theory and Local Government.* Allen and Unwin.
27. HODGE, P. (1969). 'Systems analysis and design in education: analogue or analogy? *Scot. Ed. Studs.*, 1 (3), 47–57.
28. HOWELL, D.A. (1976). 'Systems analysis and

academic decision-making in universities,' *Ed. Adm.* 4 (2), 41–59.
29. LOCKE, M. (1974). *Power and Politics in the School System: a guidebook.* London: Routledge and Kegan Paul.
30. MOODIE, G.C. and EUSTACE, R. (1971). 'British universities as political systems,' *Pol. Studs.*, XIX, 294–302.
31. PATEMAN, C. (1970). *Participation and Democratic Theory.* Cambridge University Press.
32. SHARPE, L.J. (1970). 'Theories and values of local government,' *Pol. Studs.*, XVIII, 153–74.

1(d) *Administrative Theory*
33. BAKER, R.J.S. (1972). *Administrative Theory and Public Administration.* Hutchinson.
34. BROWN, R.G.S. (1970). *The Administrative Process in Britain.* Methuen.
35. DONNISON, D.V. and others (1965, 1975). *Social Policy and Administration.* Allen and Unwin.
36. DUNSIRE, A. (1973). *Administration: the word and the science.* Martin Robertson.
37. HARTLEY, O.A. (1973). 'The functions in local government: a study in theory and practice,' *Loc. Govt. Studs.*, 4, 27–40.
38. HILL, M.J. (1972). *The Sociology of Public Administration.* London: Weidenfeld and Nicholson.
39. HOWELL, D.A. (1974). 'Public administration and educational administration,' *Ed. Adm. (Bull).*, II, (2), 32–37.
40. OPEN UNIVERSITY COURSE TEAM (1974). *Approaches to the Study of Public Administration.* D331. 1) The formal structural approach, 2) the administrative process as a decision-making and goal attaining system, 3) The administrative process as incrementalism. Milton Keynes: O.U. Press.
41. SELF, P.J.O. (1972). *Administrative Theories and Politics.* Allen and Unwin.
42. STACEY, F. (1975). *British Government 1966–1975 Years of Reform.* Oxford University Press.

1(e) *Management*

43. DAVIES, J.L. (1972). 'Management objectives in LEAs and educational institutions,' (1) *Ed. Adm. (Bull).* 1 (1), 10–16 (2) *Ed. Adm. (Bull).* 2 (1), 38–54.

44. DOBSON, N. and others (eds) (1975). *Management in Education: some techniques and systems.* London: Ward Lock.

45. GLENDINNING, J.W. and BULLOCK, R.E.H. (1973). *Management by Objectives in Local Government.* Charles Knight.

46. GRAY, H.L. (1972). 'Management in education,' *J. Moral Ed.,* 1 (2), 87–95.

47. HARRIES, T.W. (1974). 'Management by objectives: a rational approach and a comparative framework approach,' *Ed. Adm. (Bull).,* 3 (1), 42–57.

48. HOUGHTON, V.P. and GEAR, A.G. (1974). 'Management science and recurrent education,' *Ed. Adm. (Bull).,* 3 (1), 13–25.

49. HOUGHTON, V. and others (eds) (1975). *Management in education: management of organizations and individuals.* Ward Lock Educational.

50. HUGHES, M.G. (ed.) (1970). *Secondary school administration: a management approach.* Oxford: Pergamon.

51. KEELING, D. (1972). *Management in government.* Allen and Unwin.

52. LOCAL GOVERNMENT OPERATIONAL RESEARCH UNIT (1966). The scope for operational research in local education administration: a report for O.E.C.D. The Unit, (Reading).

53. OPEN UNIVERSITY COURSE TEAM (1976). Management in Education E321

  Unit .1. Management in education –
      dissimilar or congruent?
  Unit 2. A case study in management –
      Sidney Stringer school and
      community college
  Unit 3. Schools as organizations
   4–5. The management of innovation in schools.

Unit	6.	Organization development: the case of Sheldon High School
Unit	7.	The role of objectives
Unit	8.	Costs in education: university examples
Unit	9.	School timetabling
Unit	10.	Planning models in education
Unit	11.	Decision analysis in education
Unit	12.	Management and the Academic Board in Further Education Colleges
Unit	13.	Management — some cultural perspectives
Unit	14.	Role, the educational manager and the individual in the organizations
Unit	15.	The manager and groups in the organizations
Unit	16.	The rationale of resource allocation

Milton Keynes,
Open University Press.

54. PADLEY J. (1972). 'Management and decision-making in Universities: a quantitative approach: *Ed. Adm. (Bull).* I 1 17–21.
See also: 4h, 5a

1(f) *Decision-making*
55. EGGLESTON, S.J. (1973). 'Decision-making on the school curriculum: a conflict model,' *Sociol.* 7 (3), 377–94.
56. LEVIN, P.H. (1972). 'On decisions and decision-making,' *Pub. Adm.*, 50, 19–44.
57. OPEN UNIVERSITY COURSE TEAM. (1974) 'Decision-making in British educational systems' E221

    1) Introduction to decision-making in education
    2) Central government of education 1 and 2
    3) Local government of education
    4) Politics, philosophy and economics in education
    5) Decision-making in the school

6)   Community involvement in
      decision-making
7)   Decision-making in post school
      education
8)   Introduction to planning and
      decision models
9)   Recurrent education — an alternative
      future?

Milton Keynes
O.U. Press

58. VICKERS (Sir) G. (1965). *The art of judgment.*
     Chapman and Hall.

1(g) *Sociology*

59. BROWN, R. (ed.) (1973). *Knowledge, educational and cultural change.* Tavistock.
60. ELDRIDGE, J.E.T. and CROMBIE, A.D. (1974). *A sociology of organizations.* Allen and Unwin.
61. MUSGROVE, F. and TAYLOR, P.M. (1969) *Society and the teacher's role.* Routledge and Kegan Paul.
62. NOBLE, T. and PYM, B. (1970). 'Collegial authority and the receding laws of power,' *Br. J. Sociol.* XXI (4), 431—45.
63. SMITH, E. and STOCKMAN, N. (1972). 'Some suggestions for a sociological approach to the study of Government reports,' *Sociol. Rev.* 20 (1), 59—77.
64. WILSON, B.R. (1962). 'The teacher's role: a sociological analysis', *Br. J. Sociol.* 13, 15—32.
65. YOUNG, M.F.D. (ed) (1971). *Knowledge and control: new directions for the sociology of education.* Collier—Macmillan.

Policy-making

2(a) *General*

66. BOADEN, N. (1971). *Urban Policy-making.* Cambridge University
67. BOYLE (Sir) E. (1965). *et al.,* 'Who are the policy-makers?,' *Pub. Adm.* 43, 251—88.

68. BURGESS, T. (1975). 'Education: retrenchment in reform,' *N. Soc.* 31 (644), 310–2.
69. CORBETT, A. (1971). 'Innovation in Education in England,' Paris: Centre for Educational Research and Innovation.
70. FOWLER, G., MORRIS, V. and OZGA, J. (Eds) (1973). *Decision-making in British Education.* Heinemann/Open Univ. Press.
71. KING, R. (1970). 'Recent Developments in Education – a survey,' *Soc. Econ. Adm.*, 4 (4), 247–78.
72. KOGAN, M. (1975). *Educational policy-making: a study of interest groups and Parliament.* Allen and Unwin.
73. KOGAN, M. (1971). *The politics of education.* Harmondsworth, Penguin Books.
74. ORGANIZATION FOR ECONOMIC CO-OPERATION AND DEVELOPMENT (1975). 'Review of national policies for education: educational development strategy in England and Wales.' O.E.C.D. (Paris).
75. TAYLOR, W. (1971). 'Alternative futures in education', *Br. J. Ed. Technol.* 2 (2), 124–36.
76. TAYLOR, W. (1976). 'Innovation without growth', *Ed. Adm.*, 4, (2), 1–13.
77. WHITE, L.F.W. (1966). 'Priorities in education', *N. Soc.* 185, 9–11.

2(b) *Committees and Commissions*
78. BAGNALL, N. (1975). 'Education and reports,' *N. Soc.* 31 (643), 387–8.
79. BOYLE, Lord (1972). 'Ministries and educational reports,' *Univs. Qu.* 27 (1), (3–10).
80. CHAPMAN, R.A. (Ed.) (1973). *The role of commissions in policy-making.* Allen and Unwin.
81. KOGAN, M. and PACKWOOD, T. (1974). *Advisory councils and committees in education.* Routledge.
82. ROYAL COMMISSION ON LOCAL GOVERNMENT IN ENGLAND (1968). (Chairman: Lord Redcliffe-Maud) Report Vol. 1. Appendices Vols. 2–3 HMSO.
83. COMMITTEE ON THE CIVIL SERVICE (1968).

(Chairman: Lord Fulton) Report (Vol. 1) and Appendices (Vols. 2–3) HMSO.

84. COMMITTEE ON HIGHER EDUCATION (1963). (Chairman: Lord Robbins) Report and Appendices A–F. HMSO.

85. COMMITTEE ON LOCAL AUTHORITY AND ALLIED PERSONAL SOCIAL SERVICES. (1968). (Chairman: F. Seebohm) Report HMSO.

86. DEPARTMENT OF EDUCATION AND SCIENCE, CENTRAL ADVISORY COUNCIL FOR EDUCATION. (1967). Children and their primary schools. A report of the Council (Chairman: Lady Plowden) Vols. 1–2. HMSO.

87. DEPARTMENT OF EDUCATION AND SCIENCE CENTRAL ADVISORY COUNCIL FOR EDUCATION (WALES) (1967). (Chairman: C.E. Gittins) Primary Education in Wales. HMSO.

88. DEPARTMENT OF EDUCATION AND SCIENCE: COMMITTEE OF ENQUIRY INTO ADULT EDUCATION. (1973). (Chairman: Sir L. Russell). Adult education: a plan for development. HMSO.

89. DEPARTMENT OF EDUCATION AND SCIENCE: COMMITTEE OF ENQUIRY INTO THE TEACHING OF READING. (1975). A language for life: Report of the committee of enquiry appointed by the Secretary of State for Education and Science under the chairmanship of Sir Alan Bullock. HMSO.

89A DES/WELSH OFFICE. A new partnership for our schools: Report of the Committee on school government (Chairman: T. Taylor). HMSO 1977.

90. DEPARTMENT OF EDUCATION AND SCIENCE: PUBLIC SCHOOLS COMMISSION. (1968). 1st Report Vols 1–2 (Chairman: Sir J. Newsom). HMSO. (1970). 2nd Report Vols 1–2 (Chairman: D.V. Donnison) HMSO.

91. DEPARTMENT OF EDUCATION AND SCIENCE. (1960). The youth service in England and Wales: Report of Committee of Enquiry of Secretary of

State for Education and Science. (Chairman: Lady Albemarle) HMSO.

92. DEPARTMENT OF EDUCATION AND SCIENCE. (1970). A Teaching Council for England and Wales: Report of the working party (Chairman: T.R Weaver). HMSO.

93. DEPARTMENT OF EDUCATION AND SCIENCE. (1972). Teacher Education and training: a report of the committee. Chairmanship: Lord James. HMSO.

94. DEPARTMENT OF THE ENVIRONMENT. (1976). Local government finance: Report of the Committee of Enquiry (Chairman: F. Layfield). HMSO.

95. EDUCATION. (6.12.74). 'The evidence of the Association of Education Committees of Enquiry into Local Government Finance,' *Education* Supplement i–iv.

96. GOSDEN, P.H.J.H. (1969). 'The Report of the Royal Commission on Local Government and the Education Service,' *J. of Ed. Adm.* Hist. II–1. 49–52.

97. HICKS, D. (1974). 'The National Advisory Council on the Training and Supply of Teachers, 1949–65,' *Br. J. Ed. Studs.* XXII (3), 249–60.

98. MINISTRY OF EDUCATION. (1964). Report of the working party (Chairman: Sir J. Lockwood) on the schools' curricula and organizations. HMSO.

99. MINISTRY OF EDUCATION: CENTRAL ADVISORY COUNCIL FOR EDUCATION. (Chairman Sir J. Newsom). (1963). Report: Half our future HMSO.

100. MINISTRY OF EDUCATION: NATIONAL ADVISORY COUNCIL ON THE TRAINING AND SUPPLY OF TEACHERS. (1962). Seventh Report: The demand and supply of teachers 1960–80. HMSO.

101. MINISTRY OF EDUCATION: SECONDARY SCHOOL EXAMINATIONS COUNCIL (Chairman: R. Beloe). (1960). Secondary school examinations other than the G.C.E. HMSO.

102.   MINISTRY OF EDUCATION AND SCOTTISH EDU-CATION DEPT. (1960). Grants to students. Report of committee (Chairman Sir C. Anderson). HMSO.

103.   MINISTRY OF HOUSING AND LOCAL GOVERN-MENT (1967). Committee on the Management of Local Government (Chairman: Sir J. Maud) Report and Appendices 1–5 HMSO.

104.   CORBETT, A. (1967). *Much Ado about education*: a critical survey of the major educational reports Council for Educational Advance.

105.   SELF, P. (1962). The Herbert Report and the values of Local Government. *Pol. Studs. X* 146–62.

See also 63

2(c) *Planning and Financial Control*

106.   ARMITAGE, P., SMITH, L.S. and ALDER, P. (1969). *Decision models for educational planning.* Allen Lane.

107.   BIRLEY, D. (1972). *Planning and education.* Routledge.

108.   COLLINS, E.A. (1966). 'The functional approach to public expenditure,' *Pub. Adm.* 44 295–313.

109.   HECLO, H. and WILDAVSKY, A. (1974). *The private government of public money.* Macmillan.

110.   OLLERENSHAW, K. (1972). *Manpower planning – the threat or spur to education.* B.A.C.I.E.

111.   RICHMOND, W.K. (1966). *Educational planning: old and new perspectives.* Joseph.

112.   REDFERN, P. (1967). *Input–output analysis and its application to education and manpower planning.* HMSO.

113.   VAIZEY, J. (1961). 'Education and manpower,' *Br. J. Ed. Studs.* X. 85–8.

114.   VAIZEY, J.E. (1963). *'The control of education'.* Faber.

115.   VAIZEY, J. and SHEEHAN, J. (1968). *Resources for education.* Allen and Unwin.

116.   WILLIAMS, G.L. (1972). What educational planning is about. *Higher Ed.* 1 (4), 381–90.

117. WOODHALL, M. (1972). *Economic aspects of education.* Slough, NFER Publishing Co.
See also 206, 210

Specific Policies

2(d)(i) *Secondary Reorganization*
118. BENN, C. and SIMON, B. (1972). *Halfway there: report on the British comprehensive school reform (2nd ed.)* Harmondsworth Penguin Edn. Books.
119. BILSKI, R. (1973). Ideology and the comprehensive schools,' *Pol. Qu.* 44 (2), 197–211.
120. BOADEN, N.T. (1971). 'Innovation, and change in English local government,' *Pol. Studs.* XIX 416–29.
121. BOYLE, Lord. (1972). 'The politics of secondary school reorganization: some reflections,' *J. Ed. Adm. Hist.*, IV–(2), 28–38.
122. FENWICK, I.G.K. (1976). *The Comprehensive school 1944–70:* the politics of secondary school reorganization. Methuen.
123. GRIFFITHS, A. (1971). *Secondary school reorganization in England and Wales.* Routledge.
124. HALSALL, E. (1973). *The comprehensive school: guidelines for the reorganization of secondary education.* Oxford, Pergamon.
125. RUBINSTEIN, D. and SIMON, B. (1973). *The evolution of the comprehensive school 1962–72.* Routledge.
See also 4j (i)

2(d)(ii) *Teacher Training*
126. BURGESS, T. (ed.) (1971). *Dear Lord James: a critique of teacher education.* Harmondsworth Penguin Books.
127. LUKES, J.R. (1975). Government policy over higher education. *Asp. Ed.* 18, 48–101.
128. WARREN, C.F. (1973). 'The 'evidence' for James,' *Ed. f. Teaching* 90, 37–45.

129. WILLEY, F.T. and MADDISON, R.E. (1971). *An enquiry into teacher training.* University of London Press.
See also 96

2(d)(iii) *The Binary System*
130. LUKES, J.R. (1967). 'The Binary Policy: a critical study.' *Univs. Qu.* 22–1, 6–46.
131. TROW, M. (1969). 'Binary dilemmas – an American view,' *Higher Ed. Rev.* Vol. 1–3, 27–43.
132. VENABLES, (Sir) P. (1965). 'Dualism in Higher Education,' *Univs. Qu.* 20–(1), 16–29.
See also 6c i) 6d

2(d)(iv) *Others*
133. TIBBLE, J.W. (Ed.) (1970). *The extra year: the raising of the school-leaving age.* Routledge.
134. JOHNSON, C.L. (1969). 'Rationalization in Agricultural Education,' *J. Ed. Adm. Hist.* II–I. 30–35.
135. JOBLING, R.G. (1969). 'Some sociological aspects of university development in England,' *Sociol. Rev.* 17(i), 11–26.

2(e) *Political Parties*
136. BARKER, R. (1972). *Education and politics* 1900–51: a study of the Labour Party. Oxford, Clarendon Press.
137. COLLINS, J.M. (1969). 'The Labour Party and the public schools: a conflict of principles,' *Br. J. Ed. Studs.* XV11. 301–11.
138. CORBETT, A. (1969). 'The Tory Educators,' *N. Soc.* 13 (347). 785–7.
139. MACKENZIE, M.L. (1967). 'The road to the circulars – a study of the evolution of Labour Party policy with regard to the comprehensive school,' *Scot. Ed. Studs.* 1 (1), 25–33.
140. OLLERENSHAW, K. (1971). *Higher education planning and policy.* Conservative and Unionist Party.
141. PARKINSON, M. (1970). *The Labour Party and the*

organization of secondary education 1918–65. Routledge and Kegan Paul.
142. WANN, P. (1971). 'The collapse of parliamentary bipartisanship in education, 1945–52,' *J. Ed. Adm. Hist.* III.–(2), 24–34.

2(f) *Research and information*
143. GLENNERSTER, H. and HOYLE, E. (1971). 'Educational Research and education policy,' *J. Soc. Pol.* 1 (3), 193–212.
144. NEAVE, G. (1973). 'R. and D. for education in Britain and Sweden,' *Pol. Qu.* 44 (3).
145. PARKINSON, M.H. (1973). *Politics of urban education*: research report on an SSRC project into the formation of education policy in an urban setting. U. of Liverpool (Liverpool).
146. STEWART, M.A. and others. (1966). 'The role and function of educational research',
    I.   *What the teachers associations want.*
    II.   *LEAs and research.*
    III.   *Does initial training prepare teachers to understand and take part in educational research.*
147. TUNSTALL, J. (1970). 'The education correspondents', *N. Soc.* 16 (413), 366–7.
148. WALL, W.D. (1968). *Educational research and policy-making.* Slough: National Foundation for Educational Research.

Central government and control of educational systems

3(a) *General*
149. ALEXANDER, Sir W.P. (1964). *Education in England: the national system — how it works (2nd ed).* Newnes.
150. ALEXANDER, Sir W.P. (1969). *Towards a new Education Act.* Councils and Education Act.
151. BARON, G. (1965). *Schools, Society and progress in England.* Oxford: Pergamon Press.
152. BELL, R. (1973). *Education in Great Britain and*

Ireland: a source book. Routledge with Open University Press.

153. BURGESS, T. (1972). *A guide to English schools.* Harmondsworth: Penguin Books.

154. DENT, H.C. (1969). *The educational system of England and Wales (4th edn.).* University of London Press.

155. EDMONDS, E.L. (1962). *The school inspector.* Routledge.

156. GOSDEN, P.H.J.H. (1966). *The development of educational administration in England and Wales.* Oxford: Blackwell.

157. KOGAN, M. (1971). *The government of education.* Basingstoke: Macmillan education.

158. LAWRENCE, B. (1972). *The administration of education in Britain.* Batsford.

159. LESTER SMITH W.O. (1968). *Government of education (2nd Ed.).* Harmondsworth: Penguin Books.

160. ORGANIZATION FOR ECONOMIC COOPERATION AND DEVELOPMENT (O.E.C.D.) (1972). Classification of educational systems in OECD member countries. United Kingdom; England and Wales, Northern Ireland, Scotland. Paris, OECD.

161. OWEN. J.G. (1970). 'The administration of education: a decade of inevitable change,' *S.W. Rev. Pub. Adm.* 41—46.

162. PARRY, J.P. (1971). *The provision of education in England and Wales: an introduction.* Allen and Unwin.

163. PEDLEY, F.H. (1964). *The educational system in England and Wales.* Oxford: Pergamon Press.

164. PRATT, J. and others. (1973). *Your local education.* Harmondsworth: Penguin Books.

165. RAISON, T. (1976). *The Act and the partnership.* Bedford Square Press.

166. SILVER, H. (1966). 'Education and the working of democracy,' *Tech. Ed.* 8, 204—5, 268—9.

167. STANYER, J. (1976). *Understanding local government.* Fontana/Collins.

168. STANYER, J. and SMITH, B. (1976). *Administering*

Britain. Fontana/Collins.
169. STEEL, D.R. and STANYER, J. (1975). 'Administrative developments in 1973 and 1974: a survey,' *Pub. Adm.* 53, 241—86.
170. WEST, E.G. (1970). *Education and the state: a study in political economy (2nd ed.)*. Institute of Economic Affairs.
171. WRIGHT, M. (1973). 'The professional conduct of civil servants,' *Pub. Adm.* 51, 1—16.
See also 4b

3(b) *Legal Aspects*
172. BARRELL, G.R. (1970). *Legal cases for teachers*. Methuen.
173. BARRELL, G.R. (1975). *Teachers and the law (4th edn)*. Methuen.
174. BEVAN, H.K. (1973). *The law relating to children*. Butterworth.
175. DENT, H.C. (1972). *The Education Act 1944 (etc.) 12th edn*. University of London Press.
176. ELGIN, H. (1967). *The law and the teacher*. Ward Lock.
177. MATTISON, F.T. (1973). 'The Industrial Relations Act 1971 and the Universities,' *J. Ed. Adm. Hist.* VII (2), 40—44.
178. PARTINGTON, J.A. (1975). 'Secondary reorganization and the Courts of Law,' *J. Ed. Adm. Hist.* VII (2), 40—44.
179. TAYLOR, G. and SAUNDERS, J.B. (1971). *The new law of education (7th edn)*. Butterworths.

3(c) *Parliament*
180. BARKER, A. and RUSH, M. (1970). *The Member of Parliament and his information*. Allen and Unwin.
181. BOYLE (Sir) E. (1966—67). Parliament and University Policy. *Min.* 5. 1—19.
182. BUTT, R. (1969). *The power of Parliament (2nd edn.)*. Constable.
183. COHEN, L.H. (1973). Local government complaints: the M.P.'s viewpoint. *Pub. Adm.* 51, 175—83.

184. HOUSE OF COMMONS: COMMITTEE ON PUBLIC ACCOUNTS. (1967). Parliament and control of university expenditure: special report 1966—67. HMSO.

185. HOUSE OF COMMONS: EXPENDITURE COMMITTEE. (1973). Report from Education and the Arts sub-committee 1972—3. Further and Higher Education Vol. 1 — Report. Vols. 2—3 Evidence. HMSO.

186. HOUSE OF COMMONS: EXPENDITURE COMMITTEE. (1974). 3rd Report, session 1974 Educational maintenance allowances in the 16—18 years age group. HMSO.

187. HOUSE OF COMMONS: EXPENDITURE COMMITTEE. (1976). Tenth Report Session 1975—6. Policy-making in the Department of Education and Science. HMSO.

188. HOUSE OF COMMONS: SELECT COMMITTEE ON EDUCATION AND SCIENCE. (1968). Report 1967—8 Pts. I and II.
Pt. I Her Majesty's Inspectorate (England and Wales).
Pt.II Her Majesty's Inspectorate (Scotland). HMSO.

189. HOUSE OF COMMONS: SELECT COMMITTEE ON EDUCATION AND SCIENCE. (1969). Student relations: report and evidence. HMSO.

190. HOUSE OF COMMONS: SELECT COMMITTEE ON EDUCATION AND SCIENCE. (1970). Teacher Training, Session 1969—70. Evidence and appendices. HMSO.

191. HOUSE OF COMMONS: SELECT COMMITTEE ON RACE RELATIONS AND IMMIGRATION. (1969). The problems of coloured school-leavers. Report Vols. 1—2. HMSO.

192. HOUSE OF COMMONS: SELECT COMMITTEE ON RACE RELATIONS AND IMMIGRATION. (1972). Special reports 1971—2. 1st report: Statistics of immigrant school pupils. HMSO.

193. JOHNSON, N. (1961). 'Parliamentary questions and the conduct of administration,' *Pub. Adm.* 39, 131—48.

194. KOGAN, M. (1969). 'Audit, control and freedom,' *Higher Ed. Rev.* 1–2, 16–27.
195. MERRISON, A. (1975). 'The education of Ministers of State,' *(New) Univs. Qu.* 30, 2–14.
196. RICHARDS, P.G. (1972). *The backbenchers.* Faber.
197. SHELL, D.R. (1969–70). 'Specialist Select Committees,' *Parl. Aff.* 23. 380–404.
198. WALKLAND, S.A. (1968–9). 'The Public Accounts Committee the UGC and the Universities,' *Parl. Aff.* 22, 349–60.
See also 72

3(d) *Ministers*
199. BOYLE (Sir) E. and CROSLAND, A. (1971). *The Politics of Education.* Harmondsworth: Penguin Books.
200. BUTLER, Lord. (1971). *The art of the possible.* Hamish Hamilton.
201. GORDON-WALKER, P.C. (1972). The Cabinet (2nd edn.). Fontana.
See also 72, 195

3(e) *Department of Education and Science*
202. ARMITAGE, P. (1973). 'The White Paper – a step into the dark?,' *Higher Ed. Rev.* 5–2, 3–25.
203. BURGESS, T. (1963). 'The Ministry of Education', *N. Soc.* (50), 12–13.
204. BURGESS, T. (1970). 'Try again, D.E.S.,' *N. Soc.* 15 (395), 689–90.
205. DEPARTMENT OF EDUCATION AND SCIENCE. (1972). Education: a framework for expansion (Cmnd. 5174). HMSO.
206. DEPARTMENT OF EDUCATION AND SCIENCE. (1970). Output budgetting for the Department of Education and Science: Education Planning Paper No. 1. HMSO.
207. DEPARTMENT OF EDUCATION AND SCIENCE. (1965). A plan for polytechnics and other colleges: higher education in the further educational system. (Cmnd. 3008). HMSO.

208. LUKES, J.R. (1975). 'Power and policy at the DES: a case study,' *Univs. Qu.* 29 (2), 133—65.
209. MEDLICOTT, P. (1974). 'Education in Whitehall: how the DES works,' *N. Soc.* 29 (620), 472—4.
210. PILE, Sir W. (1974). 'Corporate planning for education in the DES,' *Pub. Adm.* 52, 13—26.
211. BLACKIE, J. (1970). *Inspecting and the Inspectorate.* Routledge and Kegan Paul.
212. CORBETT, A. (1966). 'The HMIs evolve,' *N. Soc.* 8 (219), 872—3.
213. EDMONDS, E.L. (1970). 'The newly-appointed Inspector of Schools: an aspect of management,' *Br. J. Ed. Studs.* XVIII, 295—303.
214. HARTLEY, O.A. (1972). 'Inspectorates in British Central Government,' *Pub. Adm.* 50, 447—66.
See also 127, 130, 171, 187, 188

3(f) *Central—local relations*

215. BOADEN, N. (1970). 'Central Departments and Local Authorities:— The relationship examined,' *Pol. Studs.* XVIII, 175—86.
216. BRAND, J.A. (1965). 'Ministerial contrml and local autonomy in education,' *Pol. Qu.* 36 (2), 154—63.
217. GRIFFITH, J.A.G. (1966). *Central departments and local authorities.* Allen and Unwin.
218. HARTLEY, O.A. (1971). 'The relationship between central and local authorities,' *Pub. Adm.* 49, 439—56.
See also 4a: 165.

3(g) *Salaries*

219. ALEXANDER, Sir W.P. The Burnham primary and secondary schools report: a commentary (various dates).
Report 1961, 1967, 1969, 1971, 1972, 1973.
Councils and Education Press 1961, 1968, 1969, 1971, 1972, 1973.
220. ALEXANDER, Sir W.P. (1965), (1969). Commentaries on three salary reports 1969. Councils and Education Press. Commentaries on three salary reports

(1969) Councils and Education Press.
221. DEPARTMENT OF EDUCATION AND SCIENCE. Scales of salaries for teachers in primary and secondary schools for England and Wales. HMSO annually.
222. DEPARTMENT OF EDUCATION AND SCIENCE. Scales of salaries for teachers in establishments for further education, England and Wales. HMSO annually.
223. DEPARTMENT OF EDUCATION AND SCIENCE: COMMITTEE ON SCALES OF SALARIES FOR THE TEACHING STAFF OF COLLEGES OF EDUCATION. Reports. HMSO, various dates.
224. DEPARTMENT OF EDUCATION AND SCIENCE/ SCOTTISH EDN. DEPT. COMMITTEE OF ENQUIRY INTO THE PAY OF NON-UNIVERSITY TEACHERS. (1974). (Chairman: Lord Houghton of Sowerby). Report. HMSO.
225. MINISTRY OF EDUCATION (later DEPARTMENT OF EDUCATION AND SCIENCE). Report(s) of the Burnham Committee on scales of salaries for teachers in primary and secondary schools in England and Wales. HMSO, various dates.
226. EDUCATION DIGEST (20.9.74). 'The Association of Education Committee's evidence to the Houghton Committee,' *Education*, Supplement i—iv.
227. EDUCATION DIGEST (15.9.72). 'Burnham negotiations,' *Education*, i—viii.
228. NATIONAL BOARD FOR PRICES AND INCOMES. (1968 and 1969). Standing reference on the pay of university teachers in Great Britain. 1st Report HMSO. 2nd Report HMSO.
229. ROBINSON, E.E. and JAYNES, D. (1968). 'Pay and the academics,' *Higher Ed. Rev.* I:1, 39—54.

Other national agencies

3(h) i) *Parliamentary Commissioner for Administration*
230. CHINKIN, C.M. and BAILEY, R.J. (1976). 'The local Ombudsman,' *Pub. Adm.* 54, 267—82.

231. COMMISSION FOR LOCAL ADMINISTRATION IN ENGLAND. (1975/6). Reports 1975/6. HMSO.
232. DRAKE, C.D. (1970). 'Ombudsmen for local government', *Pub. Adm.* 48, 179—89.
233. PARLIAMENTARY COMMISSIONER FOR ADMINISTRATION. Annual Reports 1967—8 onwards. HMSO, various dates.

3(h) ii) *Schools Council*
234. BELL, R. and PRECOTT, W. (eds.) (1975). *The Schools Council: a second look*. Ward Lock. 1975.
235. CASTON, G. (1971). 'The Schools Council in context,' *J. Curr. Studs.* 3(i), p. 50—64.
236. KERR, J.F. and others. (1966). 'The Schools Council at work,' *Forum* 9 (i), 10—23.
237. RICHARDS, C. (1974). 'The Schools Council — an initial examination,' *Univs. Qu.* 28, (3), 323—37.

3(h) iii) *Council for National Academic Awards/Regional Advisory Councils*
238. CHAMBERS, P. (1975). 'Course validation and curriculum innovation: a critique of the influence of the CNAA on the Colleges of Education,' *Ed. f. Teaching*, 97, 2—11.
239. CORBETT, A. (1971). 'Degrees of esteem,' *N. Soc.* 18, (480), 1142—4.
240. JENKINSON, A.J. (1968). Planning in further Education: can Regional Advisory Councils do it?' *Voc. Asp. Ed.* 45, 71—77.

3(h) iv) *University Grants Committee*
241. AITKEN, (Sir) R. (1969). 'The Vice-Chancellors' Committee and the UGC,' *Univs. Qu.* 23 (2), 165—71.
242. BELOFF, M. (1967). 'British Universities and the public purse,' *Min.* V, 520—32.
243. BOWRA (Sir) M. (1969). 'UGC or Ministry?' *Univs. Qu.* 23 (2), 149—54.
244. CAINE (Sir) S. (1966). 'Universities and the State,' *Pol. Qu.* 37, 237—54.
245. GRIFFITHS, R.C. (1969). 'UGC logistical planning,'

Univ. Qu. 23 (2), 155–64.
246. HALLETT, G. (1969). 'Universities and the State,': a lecturer's view,' *Pol. Qu.* 40, 163–72.
247. HALSEY, A.H. (1969). 'The universities and the State,' *Univs. Qu.* 23 (2), 128–4.
248. JAMES, I.T. (1975). 'The University Grants Committee,' *Asp. Ed.* 18, 117–26.
249. MORRIS, A. (1974). 'Changing the ways of allocating resources to universities,' *Higher Ed. Rev.* 7(i), 18–36.
250. PRATT, J. (1975). 'The UGC Department,' *Higher Ed. Rev.* 7 (2), 19–32.
251. UNIVERSITY GRANTS COMMITTEE. Annual Survey: academic year 1963–4 and onwards. HMSO annually from 1965.
252. UNIVERSITY GRANTS COMMITTEE. Returns from universities and university colleges in receipt of Exchequer grant, academic years 1960–1 onwards. HMSO annually.
253. UNIVERSITY GRANTS COMMITTEE. (1968). University development 1962–7. HMSO.
254. UNIVERSITY GRANTS COMMITTEE. (1974). University development 1967–1972. HMSO.
See also 6f i–ii

Local Education Authorities

4(a) *General*

255. BOGDANOR, V. (1976). 'Freedom in education,' *Pol. Qu.* 47 (2), 149–59.
256. BUXTON, R.J. (1973). *Local government (2nd edition).* Harmondsworth: Penguin Books.
257. CORBETT, A. (1970). 'Is London education too big?', *N. Soc.* 16 (429), 1080–4.
258. COUSINS, P.F. (1976). 'Voluntary organisations and local government in three South London Boroughs,' *Pub. Adm.* 55, 63–82.
259. EDMONDS, E.L. (1969). 'Local education authorities present and future,' *Asp. Ed.* 9, 46–57.
260. HARROP, K.J. (1976). 'Education in the North – a

regional profile and comparison with other regions, Pt. 1 — Schools,' *Dur. Res. Rev.* VIII (37), 1—13.

261. MASON, S.C. (1970). *In our experience; the changing schools of Leicestershire.* Longman.

261A. REGAN, D.E. (1977). *Local government and education.* Allen and Unwin.

262. RHODES, G. (1972). *The new government of London: the first five years.* Weidenfeld.

263. RHODES, G. (1970). *The government of London: the struggle for reform.* Weidenfeld.

264. RUCK, S.K. and RHODES, G. (1970) *The government of Greater London.* Allen and Unwin.

See also 3(f); 96, 103, 167.

4(b) *The Education Service*

265. BIRLEY, D. (1970). *The Education Officer and his world.* Routledge and Kegan Paul.

266. BOYNTON, J.K. and others. (1975). Local Government and the Education Service. Proceedings of the fourth annual conference of the British Educational Administration Society, Winter 1975, 3—18. Cardiff, the Society.

267. GUPTA, S. (1964). 'County Delegation in Education,' *Dur. Res. Rev.* 4 (15), 152—65.

268. KOGAN, M. (1973). *County Hall: LEA.* Harmondsworth: Penguin Books.

269. LAWRENCE, D.A.E. (1970). 'The place of the divisional executive officer in educational administration,' *S.W. Rev. Pub. Adm.,* 7, 33—39.

270. LAWRENCE, D.A.E. (1968). 'Why divisional executives in Education?,' *S.W. Rev. Pub. Adm.* 5, 45—51.

271. LESSE, J. (1967). 'Tertiary Education and local government,' *Tech. Ed.,* (9—2), 66—68.

272. TAYLOR, B. (1975). Comparisons between types of institution in an LEA in 'Participation Accountability and Decision-making at Institutional level' Proceedings of the third annual conference of the British Educational Administration Society. Blagdon, BEAS.

See also 3a; 29, 96, 155

4(c) *Councillors and committees*
273. BENN, C. (1974). 'Education in committee,' *N. Soc.* 27 (595), 507–8.
274. HAMPTON, W. (1972). 'Political attitudes to changes in city council administration,' *Loc. Govt. Studs.* 2, 23–26.
275. HECLO, H.H. (1969). 'The Councillor's job,' *Pub. Adm.* 47, 185–202.
276. JONES, G.W. (1973). 'The functions and organization of Councillors,' *Pub. Adm.* 51, 135–46.
277. OLLERENSHAW, K. (1962). 'Sharing responsibility,' *Pub. Adm.* 40, 43–52.
278. REDCLIFFE-MAUD (Lord). (1967). 'Local governors at work. Could they do better?,' *Pub. Adm.* 45, 347–52.
279. SELF, P. (1971). 'Elected representatives and management in local government: an alternative analysis,' *Pub. Adm.* 49, 269–78.
280. SHARPE, L.J. (1962). 'Elected representatives in local government,' *Br. J. Sociol.* XIII (3), 189–209.
281. STANYER, J. (1971). 'Elected representatives and management in local government,' *Pub. Adm.* 49, 73–79.
282. TARAS, R. (1972). 'Communications and press relations in local government,' *Pol. Polt.* 1 (2), 115–30.
283. WISEMAN, H.V. (1963). The working of local government in Leeds. I – 'Party control of Council and Committees,' *Pub. Adm.* 41, 51–70. II – 'More party conventions and practices,' *Pub. Adm.* 41, 137–56.

4(d) *Policy Making*
284. BRIER, A.P. (1970). 'The decision process in local government; a case study,' *Pub. Adm.* 48, 153–68.
285. PESCHECK, D. and BRAND, J.A. (1966). Policies and politics in secondary education. London School of Economics.
286. CHESTER, D.N. (1968). 'Local democracy and the internal organization of local authorities,' *Pub. Adm.* 46, 287–98.

287. GREENWOOD, R. and others. (1972). 'The policy committee in English local government,' *Pub. Adm.* 50, 157—66.
287B. NEWTON, K. (1976). *Second city politics*. Oxford University Press.
288. SANDHAM, J.E. (June 1969). 'Local Government operations and the location of a college for training technical teachers: a case study of the interplay of varying policies and attitudes,' *J. Ed. Adm. Hist.* 1—2, 22—29.
289. SARAN, R. (1973). *Policy making in secondary education*: a case study. Oxford: Clarendon Press. 1973.
290. SARAN, R. (1967). 'Decision-making by a Local Education Authority,' *Pub. Adm.* 45, 387—402.

4(e) *Finance*

291. CRISPIN, A. (1976). 'Local government finance: assessing the Central Government's contribution,' *Pub. Adm.* 54, 45—62.
292. EDUCATION — (22.6.73). supplement. Finance in Education management. Knight, W.J. and Rendel Jones, J. *Edn.*, I—XV.
293. HEPWORTH, N.P. (1971). *The finance of Local Government* (2nd edn.). Allen and Unwin.
294. MORRIS, N. (1970, 1971). Education and the coming of the general grant. I — *Res. Ed.* 4, 49—72. II — *Res. Ed.* 5, 60—74.
295. PEACOCK, A. (ed.) (1968). *Educational finance: its sources and uses in the United Kingdom*. Edinburgh: Oliver and Boyd. 1968.
296. LEWIS, P. and ALLEMANO, R. (1972). 'Fact and fiction about the pool,' *Higher Ed. Rev.* 4 (2), 20—32.
297. PREECE, P.F.W. (1971). 'The laissez-faire finance of education,' *Br. J. Ed. Studs.* XIX, 154—62.
298. SELBY SMITH, C. (1970). *The costs of further education — British analysis*. Oxford: Pergamon.
See also 94

4(f) *Secondary Reorganisation*
299. BATLEY, P., PARRIS, H. and O'BRIEN, O. (1970). *Going comprehensive: educational policy-making in two county boroughs.* Routledge and Kegan Paul.
300. BURGESS, T. (1964). 'How to go comprehensive,' *N. Soc.* 4 (110), 2g.
301. CORBETT, A. (1970). 'Comprehensives: the tally,' *N. Soc.* 15 (385), 264–6.
302. CORBETT, A. (1968). 'A long way from comprehensive,' *N. Soc.* 12 (302).
303. ECCLES, P.R. (1974). 'Secondary reorganization in Tynemouth 1962–9,' *J. Ed. Adm. Hist.* VI (1), 35–44.
304. EGGLESTON, S.J. (1966). 'Going comprehensive,' *N. Soc.* 8 (221), 944–46.
305. HALSALL, E. (ed.) (1970). *Becoming comprehensive – case histories.* Oxford: Pergamon.
See also 2(d)(i); 178

4(g) *Disputes*
306. AULD, R. (1976). The William Tyndale Junior and Infant Schools: (Report) into the teaching organization and management of the William Tyndale Junior and Infant Schools. Inner London Education Authority.
307. BERG, L. (1968). *Risinghill – death of a comprehensive school.* Harmondsworth: Penguin Books.
308. CONSTABLE, T. (1968). 'The Risinghill Myth: School closure to sack a head', *N. Soc.* 11 (290), 868–70.
309. DEPARTMENT OF EDUCATION AND SCIENCE (1969). COMMITTEE OF INQUIRY INTO THE DISPUTE BETWEEN THE DURHAM LOCAL EDUCATION AUTHORITY and the NATIONAL ASSOCIATION OF SCHOOLMASTERS. Report HMSO.
310. DEPARTMENT OF EDUCATION AND SCIENCE (1973). COMMITTEE OF INQUIRY INTO THE DISPUTES INVOLVING TEACHERS IN THE AREA OF THE TEESSIDE L.E.A. Report HMSO.

311. ELLIS, T. and others (1976). *William Tyndale: the teachers' story*. Writers' and Readers' Publishing Co-operative.

312. GRETTON, J. and JACKSON, M. (1976). *William Tyndale: collapse of a school – or a system?* Allen and Unwin.

313. MACK, J. (1976). 'A school that failed,' *N. Soc.* 37 (720), 178–9.

4(h) *Management*
314. BROWNING, P. (1976). 'Corporate Planning: the myth and the reality,' *Ed. Adm.* 4 (2), 28–34.

315. BYRNE, E.M. (1974). *Planning and educational inequality: a study of a rationale of resource allocation*. Windsor: NFER Publishing Co.

316. DAVID, M.E. (1975). 'Approaches to organizational change in LEAs,' *Dur. Res. Rev.* VII (35), , 313. 1047–56.

316A. DAVID, M.E. (1977). *Reform, reaction and resource: the 3Rs of educational planning*. Windsor: NFER Publishing Co.

317. DAVID, M.E. and FISKE, D. (1973). 'Approaches to organizational change in LEAs,' *Ed. Adm. (Bull).* 1–2, 24–33.

318. GREENWOOD, R. and STEWART, J.D. (eds). (1974). *Corporate planning in English local government*. Charles Knight. 1974.

319. OWENS, E.E.L. (1969). 'The size, efficiency and effectiveness of LEAs,' *J. Ed. Adm. Hist.* 1–2, 30–39.

320. PESTON, M. and DAVID, M. (1963). 'Planning in local education authorities,' *Loc. Govt. Studs.* – 5 39–46.

321. PYLE, D. (1976). 'Aspects of resource allocations by local education authorities,' *Soc. Econ. Adm.* 10 (2), 106–22.

322. SOCIETY OF EDUCATION OFFICERS. (1975). *Management in the education service: challenge and response*. Routledge.

323. STEWART, J.D. (1974). 'Corporate management and

the education service,' *Ed. Adm. (Bull).* 3 (i),
1–12.
324. STEWART, J.D. (1971). *Management in local government: a viewpoint.* Charles Knight.
325. WOODHAM, J.B. (1972). 'Management and local democracy,' *Loc. Govt. Studs.* 2, 13–22.
See also 1(e)

4(j) *Local government reorganization*
326. BOGDANOR, V. (1976). 'Education, politics aand the reform of local government,' *Oxf. Rev. Ed.* 2 (i), 3–16.
327. BROWNING, P. (1972). 'Some changes in LEA administration,' *Lond. Ed. Rev.* 1 (3), 4–12.
328. DEPARTMENT OF THE ENVIRONMENT. (1972). The new local authorities: management and structure Report of a study group (Chairman: M.A. Bains) to the Secretary of State for the Environment and the local authority associations. HMSO.
329. ELCOCK, H.J. (1975). 'English local government reformed: the politics of Humberside,' *Pub. Adm.* 53, 159–68.
330. RICHARDS, P.G. (1973). *The reformed local government system.* Allen and Unwin.
331. TAYLOR, G. (1971). 'Yorkshire's educational shake-up,' *N. Soc.* 17 (449), 769–70.
See also 82

4(k) *Variation in provision*
332. ALT, J.E. (1971). 'Some social and political correlates of county borough expenditure,' *Br. J. Pol. Sci.* 1, 49–62.
333. BOADEN, N.T. and ALFORD, R.R. (1969). 'Sources of diversity in English local government decisions,' *Pub. Adm.* 47, 203–24.
334. GREENWOOD, R. and STEWART, J.D. (1973). 'Towards a typology of English local authorities,' *Pol. Studs.* XXI, 64–69.
335. KANTOR, P. (1976). 'Elites, pluralists and policy

arenas in London: towards a comparative theory of city policy formulation,' *Br. J. Pol. Sci.* 6 (3), 311–314.

See also 7c

4(l) *Buildings*
336. DEPARTMENT OF EDUCATION AND SCIENCE. (1976). The consortia: co-operation in educational building. HMSO.
337. DEPARTMENT OF EDUCATION AND SCIENCE. (1965). The school building survey 1962. HMSO.
338. EDUCATION — Supplement. (30.4.71). Consortia 1971,' *Edn.*, p. xvi.
339. EDUCATION — Supplement. (25.5.73). 'Consortia 1973', *Edn.*, 1–xx.
340. EDUCATION. (30.5.75). 'Consortia 1975', *Edn.*, Supplement 1–xvi.

Institutional administration and management schools

5(a) *School Management and Government*
341. BARON, G. and HOWELL, D.A. (1974). *The government and management of schools*. Athlone Press.
342. BARON, G. and HOWELL, D.A. (1968). School management and government, (Royal Commission on Local Government in England, Research Studies 6), HMSO.
343. EDUCATION DIGEST. (15.10.71). 'Managers and governors,' *Edn.* 1–v.
344. GLATTER, R. (1976). 'Reforming school management: some structural issues,' *Ed. Adm.* 5 (i), 50–59.
345. HOWELL, D.A. (1976). 'The government and management of schools reconsidered', *Res. Ed.* 16, 67–72.
346. KOGAN, M. and others. Institutional autonomy and public accountability; Proceedings of the Joint Annual Conference of the British Educational Administration Society, 1975. 19–37. Cardiff, The Society, 1975.
347. LAWRENCE, D.A.E. (1969). 'Managers and governors

and their role in our schools,' *S.W. Rev. Pub. Adm.* 6, 31–6.

348. PARKES, D.L. and WILLIAMS, T.A. (1973). 'Circular 7/70 and the government of schools,' *Ed. Adm. (Bull).* I, 2, 1–15.

349. ROBINSON, E. (1972). 'Governing classes,' *N. Soc.* 22 (524).

See also 1(f); 89A, 151, 153

Schools as Organizations

5(b) (i) *General*

350. DAVIES, T.I. (1969) *School organization: a new synthesis.* Oxford: Pergammon. 1969.

351. CHAPMAN, J. (1971). 'School councils in theory and practice,' *J. Moral Ed.* 1.

352. GOULD, R. (1976). 'The ecology of educational settings,' *Ed. Adm.* 4 (2) 14–27.

353. KINE, R. (1973). *School organization and pupil involvement.* Routledge and Kegan Paul.

354. MACK, J. (1976). 'Assessing Schools,' *N. Soc.* 38 (738), 401–3.

355. MUSGROVE, F. (1971). *Patterns of power and authority in English education.* Methuen.

356. MUSGROVE, F. (1973). 'Power and the integrated curriculum,' *J. Curr. Studs.* 5 (1), 3–12.

357. POSTER, C. (1976). *School decision making.* Heinemann.

358. SHAW, K.E. (1969). 'Effectiveness in educational organizations,' *J. Ed. Adm. Hist.* II (1), 42–8.

359. TAYLOR, E. (1975). 'Who rules schools?' *N. Soc.* 32 (663) 717–8.

See also 8, 24

5(b) (ii) *Educational Management*

360. BRIAULT, E.W.H. and others. (31.12.71). Supplement on education management, *Edn.* Supp. ii–vii. Distributed administration: techniques of leadership.

361. COOKE, D. and DUNHILL, J. (1963). *School organi-*

zation and management. University of London Press.

362. EDUCATION SUPPLEMENT. (15.9.72). Education management, *Edn.* i—xii WHITE, L.F.W., Preparing for making decisions in 1974. DAVIES, J.L., Why management course in Polytechnics? PACK-WOOD, G.F.L. Analysis of educational organizations.

363. EDUCATION SUPPLEMENT. (25.6.71). Education management, *Edn.* i—xx TAYLOR, W., Courses in administration for practitioners. OWEN, J., Developments in management training. BONE, T.R., Training for responsibility in education. AITKEN, R., Programme budgeting. TOMLINSON, J.R.G., Typology of middle managers.

364. ELBOIM-DROR, R. (1972). 'The management system in education and staff relations, Part I,' *J. Ed. Adm. Hist.* IV (1), 37—45. Part II IV (2), 1972, 47—56.

365. FAIRLIE, H. and others. (11.4.75). 'Education management: straws in the wind,' *Edn.* Supplement iii—viii.

366. GRAY, H.L. and BARNES, A.R. (1972). 'Training in the management of education,' *Ed. Adm. (Bull).* I 1, 1—9.

367. KOGAN, M. and others. (19.7.74). 'Education management: management and management training,' *Edn.* Supplement i—viii.

368. SHIPMAN, M.D. (1969). 'Order and innovation in schools,' *N. Soc.* 14 (377) 976—8.

369. TAYLOR, G. 'Management in education,' *Br. J. Ed. Technol.* 2 (ii) January 1971, 67—75.

370. TAYLOR, W. (ed.) *The teacher as manager.* Books for Schools, Ltd., 1970.

371. TAYLOR, W. *et. al.* (25.6.71). Education management, *Edn.* 137, Supplement v—xviii.

372. TOMLINSON, J.R.G. and others. (8.11.74). Education management: reorganization and after, *Edn.* Supplement i—xvi.

373. UMANS, S., (1972). *The management of education: a*

systematic design for educational revolution. Pitman.

5(b) (iii) *Head Teachers*

374. ALLEN, B. (Ed.), (1968). *Headship in the 1970s.* Oxford: Blackwell.

375. BARRY, C.H. and TYE, F. (1975). *Running a school.* Temple Smith.

376. BERNBAUM, G. (1973). 'Headmasters and schools: some preliminary findings,' *Sociol. Rev.* 21 (3), 463—84.

377. COOK, A. and MACK, H. (1971). *The headteacher's role.* Basingstoke: Macmillan Education.

378. CORBETT, A. (1971). 'The school bosses,' *N. Soc.* 47 (446), 627—30.

379. DALRYMPLE, A.M. (1969). 'The changing position of a headmaster,' *Br. J. Ed. Studs.* XVII, 66—82.

380. EDMUNDS, E.L. (1968). *The first headship.* Oxford: Blackwell. 1968.

381. EDUCATION. (13.4.73). Digest. 'The headteacher', *Edn.* i—viii.

382. EVANS, K. (1974). 'The head and his territory,' *N. Soc.* 30 (629), 199—201.

383. GOODWIN, F.J. (1968). *The art of the headmaster.* Ward Lock.

384. GRAY, H.L. (1973). 'The function of a head of a school,' *J. Moral. Ed.* 2 (2), 99—108.

385. GUTHRIE, R. (1969). 'How progressive can a state school be?,' *N. Soc.* 13 (332) 203—6.

386. HOYLE, E. (1972). 'Educational innovation and the role of the teacher,' *Forum* 14 (2) 42—4.

387. HUGHES, M.G. (1975). 'The innovating school head: autocratic innovator or catalyst of cooperation?' *Ed. Adm.* 4 (1) 29—47.

388. HUGHES, M.G. (1972.) 'School headship in transition,' *Lond. Ed. Rev.* I, 34—42.

389. LAWRENCE, L. (1974). 'The head and his teachers,' *N. Soc.* 30 (629) 201—03.

390. PETERS, R.S. (Ed.) (1976). *The role of the head.* Routledge.

391. SMITH, D.M. (1975). 'Points allocation, secondary schools and teachers,' *Ed. Studs.* 1 (3) 163–170.

392. SMITH, D.M. (1975). 'Headteachers' allocation of salary points in English secondary schools,' *Ed. Studs.* 1 (2) 113–119.

393. STEINMAN, M. (1973). 'Class correlates of head teachers' attitudes,' *Pol. Polt.* 1–4, 307–26.

394. TURNER, C.M. (1974.) 'The head teacher as a manager,' *J. Ed. Adm. Hist.* VI (2) 31–37.

395. WESTWOOD, L.J. (1966). 'Reassessing the role of the head,' *Ed. f. Teaching* 71, 65–74.

5(b) (iv) *Teaching Staff*

396. ASHMALL, H.A. (1975). 'Staff Manuals: an exercise in communication,' *Ed. Adm.* 4 (1) 1–10.

397. BAILEY, P. HOGAN, D. and GRAY, H.L. (1975). 'Developing staff in educational organizations: a symposium,' *Ed. Adm.* 4 (1) 11–28.

398. DAVIES, W. (1972). 'Educational Administration and the young teacher,' *Lond. Ed. Rev.* 1–3, 43–50.

399. HILSUM, S. and CANE, B. (1971). *The Teacher's day.* Slough: NFER.

400. HOGAN, D.F. and PEPPER, R. (1972). 'Staff involvement in school organization: two views,' *Lond. Ed. Rev.* 1 (3), 21–28.

401. HOYLE, E. (1969). *The Role of the Teacher.* Routledge and Kegan Paul.

402. JENNINGS, A. (1975). The participation of the teaching staff in decision-making in schools; Proceedings of the Third Annual Conference of the British Educational Administration Society, Blagdon, BEAS.

403. TURNER, B. (Ed.), (1973). *Discipline in schools.* Ward Lock. 1973.

404. VENABLES, E. (1971). *Teachers and youth workers: a study of their role.* Evans: Methuen.

405. WESTWOOD, L.J. (1967). 'The role of the teacher: I and II,' *Ed. Res.* 9 (2) Feb. 67, 122–62. *Ed. Res.* 10 (1) Nov. 67, 21–37.

5(c) *Pre-School Provision*
406. BLACKSTONE, T. (1970). 'The distribution of nursery education in England and Wales,' *Soc. Econ. Adm.* 4–1, 45–55.
407. BLACKSTONE, T. (1969). 'Where nursery schools are,' *N. Soc.* 14 (367) 560–61.
408. MACK, J. (1975). 'The pre-school drive,' *N. Soc.* 34 (687) 535–7.
See also 7(c)

5(d) *Primary Schools*
409. BLYTH, W.A.L. (1965). *English primary education Vols. 1, 2.* Routledge and Kegan Paul.
410. DEPARTMENT OF EDUCATION AND SCIENCE. (1968). Parent/teacher relations in primary schools, HMSO.
411. COULSON, A.A. (1976). 'Leadership functions in primary schools,' *Ed. Adm.* 5 (1) 37–49.
412. LYONS, G. (1966). 'Primary school,' *N. Soc.* 8 (207), 395–401.
413. PAPE, G.V. (1972). 'Running the primary schools,' *Lond. Ed. Rev.* I (3), 13–20.
414. TAYLOR, P.H. (and others). (1974). *Purpose, power and constraint in the primary school curriculum.* Basingstoke: Macmillan.
See also 86

5(e) *Secondary Schools – General*
415. BERNBAUM, G. (1973). Countesthorpe (in Case studies in educational innovation, Vol. III – at the school level), Paris, CERI (OECD).
416. HARGREAVES, D. (1967). *Social relations in a secondary school.* Routledge.
417. HEWITSON, J.N. (1969). *The grammar school tradition in a comprehensive world.* Routledge and Kegan Paul.
418. HUGHES, M.G. (1973). 'The professional as administrator: The case of the secondary school head,' *Ed. Adm. (Bull).* 2 (1), 11–23.
419. JENNINGS, A. and others. (20.6.75). 'The large

secondary school: making it work,' *Edn.* Supplement i—xii.

420. LAMBERT, K. (1975). 'The role of heads of department in schools,' *Ed. Adm. (Bull).* 3 (2), 27—39.

421. LYONS, G. (1976). *Heads' tasks: a handbook of secondary school administration.* Windsor: NFER Publishing.

422. LYONS, G. (1972). 'Patterns of administrative work in secondary schools,' *Ed. Adm. (Bull).* I (1) 22—28.

423. McDOWELL, D. (1973). 'Some organizational issues in the education of minorities,' *Lond. Ed. Rev.* 2 (1), 37—42.

424. MARLAND, M. (1974). *Pastoral care.* Heinemann Educational Books.

425. RICHARDSON, E. (1975). *Authority and organization in the secondary school.* Macmillan.

426. RICHARDSON, E. (1973). *The teacher, the school and the task of management.* Heinemann Educational Books.

427. TAYLOR, W. (1973). *Heading for change: The management of innovation in the large secondary school.* Routledge.

428. TOWNSEND, H.E.R. (1972). *Organization in multiracial schools.* Windsor: NFER. 1972.

429. WEBB, P.C. (1973—74). 'Staff development in large secondary schools,' *Ed. Adm. (Bull).* 2 (1) 1973, 24—37. *Ed. Adm. (Bull).* 2 (2) 1974, 55—62.

See also 50, 99

5(f) *Comprehensive Secondary Schools*

430. ASHMALL, H. (1976). 'Aspects of school management in a comprehensive school,' *Scot. Ed. Studs.* 8 (2) 95—105.

431. BAILEY, P. (1973). 'The functions of heads of departments in comprehensive schools,' *J. Ed. Adm. Hist.* VI, 52—58.

432. CONWAY, E.S. (1970). *Going comprehensive: a study of the administration of comprehensive schools.* Harrap.

433. FRANCIS, P. (1975). *Beyond control?: a study of*

discipline in the comprehensive school. Allen and Unwin.

434. MARLAND, M. (1971). *Head of department: teaching a department in a comprehensive school.* Heinemann Educational.
435. MEDLICOTT, P. (1974). 'Streaming in the comprehensive school,' *N. Soc.* 30 (632) 414—7.
436. MONKS, T.G. (1968). *Comprehensive education in England and Wales: a survey of schools and their organization.* Slough: NFER.
437. MONKS, T.G. (Ed.) (1970). *Comprehensive education in action,* Slough, NFER.
438. NEAVE, G. (1975). *How they fared: the impact of the comprehensive school upon the university.* Routledge.
439. ROSS, J.M. and CHANAN, G. (1972). *Comprehensive schools in focus.* Windsor: NFER.
440. ROSS, J.M. and others. (1972). *A critical appraisal of comprehensive education.* Windsor: NFER.

5(g) *Middle Schools*
441. BENN, C. (1973). 'The middle school experiment,' *N. Soc.* 23 (553) 294—6.
442. EDWARDS, R. (1972). *The middle school experiment.* Routledge and Kegan Paul. 1972.
443. GANNON, M. and WHALLEY, A. (1975). *Middle schools.* Heinemann.

5(h) *VI Form Colleges*
444. DAVID, T. (Ed.), (1972). *The sixth form college in practice.* Councils and Education Press.
445. EDUCATION Supplement. (1971). 'Sixth form colleges,' *Edn.* 1.10.71, i—xii.
446. EDWARDS, A.D. (1970). 'Exeter's sixth form solution,' *N. Soc.* 16 (408), 151—2.
447. KING, R.A. (1976). *School and college: studies in post-sixteen education.* Routledge and Kegan Paul. 1976.

5(j) *Voluntary and Private Schools*
448. BAGNALL, N. (1966). 'The direct grant schools,' *N. Soc.* 174, 20–21.
449. CORBETT, A. (1968). 'Catholics at school,' *N. Soc.* 12 (322).
450. GLENNERSTER, H. and WILSON, G. (1970). *Paying for private schools.* Allen Lane.
451. KALTON, G. (1966). *The public schools: a factual survey.* Longmans.
452. KELLY, S.E. (1971). 'The voluntary schools in four Lancashire boroughs 1903–68: A study of policies and provision.' *J. Ed. Adm. Hist.* III (2), 42–52.
453. KING, R. (1967). 'State boarding and the future of public schools,' *N. Soc.* 19 (250) 46–48.
See also 90

Institutional administration and management – higher and further education

6(a) *The further education system*
454. BRATCHELL, D.F. (1968). *The aims and organizations of further education.* Oxford: Pergamon.
455. BURGESS, T. and PRATT, J. (1971). *Case studies on innovation in higher education and technical education in the United Kingdom.* Paris: OECD.
456. CANTOR, L.M. and ROBERTS, I.F. (1972). *Further education in England and Wales (2nd edn.).* Routledge.
457. COOMBE LODGE FURTHER EDUCATION STAFF COLLEGE: REPORTS (20 per annum) Blagdon, the College, annually from 1963.
458. DEPARTMENT OF EDUCATION AND SCIENCE: *NATIONAL ADVISORY COUNCIL ON ART EDUCATION.* (1970). The structure of art and design education in the further education sector. Report (Sir W. Coldstream). HMSO.
459. LESSE, J. (1966). 'A new voice for further education,' *Tech. Ed.* 298–300.
460. LOCKE, M. (1976). *The statutory framework of further education.* Blagdon, Further Education Staff College.

461. MURIE, A. (1972). 'Industrial training and the extension of educational provision,' *Voc. Asp. Ed.* 24, 1–7.
462. PETERS, A.J. (1967). *British Further Education, a critical textbook.* Oxford: Pergamon.
463. PETERS, A.J. (1964). 'Published sources for the study of contemporary British further education,' *Br. J. Ed. Studs.* XIII, 71–86.
464. ROBINSON, E.E. (1969). 'The cuts and further education,' *Higher Ed. Rev.* I 3, 19–26.
465. SRIRENGAN, K. (1972). 'A systems approach to technician education and training,' *Voc. Asp. Ed.* 24, 23–28.
466. WELLENS, J. (1965). 'The technical college in a changing environment,' *Tech. Ed.*, 444–7.
See also 185

6(b) *FE Institutions*
467. BRIAULT, E. (1976). 'The role of the principal,' *Ed. Adm.* 4 (2), 35–40.
468. CHARLTON, D. and others. (1971). *The administration of technical colleges.* Manchester: Manchester University Press.
469. CORBETT, A. (1972). 'Kingsway College,' *N. Soc.* 22 (531), 560–63.
470. DEPARTMENT OF EDUCATION AND SCIENCE. (1969). (National advisory council for education in industry and commerce). Committee on technician courses and examinations (Chairman: H.L. Hasegrave). Report. HMSO.
471. EASTON, W.A.G. (1969). 'Analysis of a (FE) College,' *Tech. J.*

   I. 7 (1) Feb. 1969 9–10
   II 7 (2) March 1969 10–11
   III 7 (3) April 1969 7–9
   IV 7 (4) May 1969 15–16
   V 7 (5) June 1969 21–22

472. DEPARTMENT OF EDUCATION AND SCIENCE. (1970). Committee on the more effective use of technical college resources. Report of an inquiry

into the pattern and organization of the college year. HMSO.

473. DEPARTMENT OF EDUCATION AND SCIENCE. (1968). National Advisory Council on Education for Industry and Commerce. Committee on the more effective use of technical college resources. A report on the use of buildings and equipment. HMSO.

474. EDUCATION (25.5.73). – Digest 'Industrial Training', *Edn.*, i–iv.

475. MEDLICOTT, P. (1973). 'The further education vacuum cleaner,' *N. Soc.* 26 (581), 459–60.

476. HICKS, J. (1975). 'College principals and vice-principals: roles and functions,' *Ed. Adm.* 4 (1), 48–59.

477. MUMFORD, D. and others. (5.12.75). 'The management of advanced further education,' *Edn.*, Supplement i–xiv.

478. SIMMONS, D.D. (ed.) (1971). College management – readings and cases: A staff development handbook Vols. I–II. Blagdon: Further Education Staff College.

479. TIPTON, B.F.A. (1973). *Conflict and change in a technical college*. Hutchinson.

480. TIPTON, B.F.A. (1972). 'Some organizational characteristics of a technical college,' *Res. Ed.* 7, 11–27.

481. TURNER, C.M. (1975). 'The further education college as a predictable organization: power dependency analysis,' *Ed. Studs.* 1 (3), 201–208.

482. WHEELER, G.E. (1966). 'The management of colleges,' *Tech. J.* (4–4), 8–11.

See also 23

Higher Education – general

6(c) (i) *Policy*

483. ARMITAGE, P. (1962). 'Notions about numbers and the make-believe of planning', *Higher Ed. Rev.* 4 (3), 30–41.

484. ANNAN, N. (1967). 'The reform of higher education,'

Pol. Qu. 38, 234—52.

485. BROSAN, G. and others. (1971). *Patterns and policies in higher education.* Harmondsworth: Penguin Books.

486. BURGESS, T. and PRATT, J. (1970). *Policy and practice: the colleges of advanced technology.* Allen Lane.

487. BURGESS, T. (ed.) (1972). *The shape of higher education.* Cornmarket Press.

488. BURGESS, T. (ed.) (1972). *Planning for higher education.* Cornmarket Press.

489. COLLIER, K.G. (1974). *Innovation in higher education.* Windsor: NFER Publishing Co.

490. LAND, F.W. (1975). 'Planning ahead', *Asp. Ed.* 18, 26—47.

491. LAWLOR, J. (ed.) (1972). *Higher education: patterns of change in the 1970s.* Routledge.

492. MACARTHUR, B. (1970). 'Who plans higher education?', *Higher Ed. Rev.* 2 (2), 31—37.

493. MENNELL, S. and CROUCH, C. (1972). 'Autonomy and diversity in higher education,' *Univs. Qu.* 26 (4), 407—28.

494. NIBLETT, W.R. (1969). *Higher Education: demand and response.* Tavistock.

495. VAIZEY, J. (1970). 'The future of higher education', *N. Soc.* 15 (309), 866—9.

See also 84, 130, 207

6(c) (ii) *administration*

496. BEALE, R.J. (1966). 'The organizational structure of large colleges of technology', *Tech. Ed.* 8, 310—11.

497. BIRCH, D.W. and CALVERT, J.R. (1974). 'A review of academic staffing formulae', *Ed. Adm. (Bull).* 3 (1), 32—41.

498. COTGROVE, S. (1967). 'The administration of academics', *Tech. J.* 5 (6), 20—22.

499. FIELDEN, J. (1973). 'Management information in higher education. The gulf between theory and practice', *Ed. Adm. (Bull).* 1 (2), 16—23.

500. LAYARD, R. and OATEY, M. 'The cost effectiveness

of the new media in Higher Education', *Br. J. Ed. Technol.* 4 (3)

501. PRATT, J. (1976). 'Pooling: some revised conclusions', *Higher Ed. Rev.* 8 (2), 23–37.

502. WILLIAMS, G. (1974). 'Higher education deflated', *N. Soc.* 30 (633), 471–3.

See also 271

6(d) *Polytechnics*

503. ANTIA, J.M. (1976). 'Critical success factors in polytechnic performance', *Ed. Adm.* 5 (1), 14–36.

504. BROWN, I. (1971). 'The dispersed polytechnic', *Higher Ed. Rev.* 3 (2), 25–45.

505. CAMPBELL, F.J. (1974). 'High command: the making of an oligarchy at the Polytechnic of North London, 1970–74', *Time Out.*

506. DONALDSON, L. (1975). *Policy and the polytechnics; pluralistic drift in higher education.* Farnborough: Saxon House.

507. GENT, B. (1975). 'The polytechnics: Education and action', *Asp. Ed.*, 146–57.

508. JACKA, K. and others. (1975). *Rape of reason: the corruption of the Polytechnic of North London.* Enfield: Churchill Press.

509. JOHNSON, N. (1968). 'Polytechnics and inegalities', *Univs. Qu.* 23 (1), 12–16.

510. LEWIS, P. (1971). 'Finance and the fate of the polytechnics', *Higher Ed. Rev.* 3 (3), 23–34.

511. MACK, J. (1976). 'The polytechnics' unhappy birthday', *N. Soc.* 35 (694), 156–9.

512. MEDLICOTT, P. (1975). 'Polytechnics: good buy or farewell?', *N. Soc.* 31 (642), 191–2.

513. OXTOBY, R. (1971). 'Top men at the polys', *N. Soc.* 7 (439), 306–309.

514. PRATT, J. and BURGESS, T. (1974). *Polytechnics: a report.* Pitman.

515. ROBINSON, E.E. (1968). *The new polytechnics.* Cornmarket Press.

Colleges of education

6(e) (i) *policy*
516. ADCOCK, R.A. and ELLIOTT, J. (1971). The signifi-
cance of the Durham report for the Church
colleges of education. *Ed. f. Teaching* 84 28–43.
517. DEPARTMENT OF EDUCATION AND SCIENCE
(1966). Study group on the government of colleges
of education (Chairman: T.R. Weaver). HMSO.
518. EVANS, A.A. (1971). 'Colleges of education – the
next phase', *Camb. J. Ed*. No. 1, 4–15.
519. HEWETT, S. (1970). 'Changing roles for colleges of
education', *Univs. Qu.* 25 (1), 3–16.
520. HEWETT, S. (1974). 'Policy, partnership and professionalism in teacher education', *Lond. Ed. Rev.*
3 (2), 41–50.
521. HEWETT, S. (ed.) (1971). *The training of teachers: a
factual survey*. University of London Press.
522. PARRY, J.P. (1967). 'The idea of a college of education', *Ed. f. Teaching* 72, 2–19.
523. PAYNE, N.P. (1975). 'The colleges of education', *Asp.
Ed*. 18, 58–69.
524. BAGGETT, M. and CLARKSON, R. (eds.) (1976).
Changing patterns of teacher education. Falmer
Press/Ward Lock.
See also 96

6(e) (ii) *administration*
525. BRADSHAW, D.C.A. (1970). 'Diversifying colleges of
education', *Univs. Qu.* 20 (4), 392–401.
526. BURKE, V.B. (1968). 'Student participation in the
government of colleges of education', *Univs. Qu.*
22 (4), 398–403.
527. PASTON BROWN (Dame) B. (1971). 'Participation'
and college government, *Camb. J. Ed*. No. 2,
50–59.
528. PORTER, J. (1972). 'The new role of the college
principal', *Lond. Ed. Rev.*, 29–33.
529. PRICE, G. (1969). 'Economics and the size of college',
Ed. f. Teaching 79, 55–62.

530. SHAW, K.E. and DOWNES, L.W. (1971). 'Unitary and discrepant goals in a college of education', *Br. J. Ed. Studs.* XIX, 139—53.
531. SMITH, R.F. and COLLIER, K.G. (1972). 'Staffing policies in a college of education', *Univs. Qu.* 27 (1), 90—101.
532. TAYLOR, W. (1964). 'The training college principal', *Sociol. Rev.* 12 (2), 185—201.

Universities

6(f) (i) *government*
533. CARTER, C.F. and ANNAN, Lord (1966). 'The Franks report: from the outside; from the near-side', *Univs. Qu.* 20 (4), 381—406.
534. MOODIE, G.C. and EUSTACE, R. (1974). *Power and authority in British Universities.* Allen and Unwin.
535. PESTON, M. (1976). 'The education of Vice-Chancellors', *New Univs. Qu.* 30 (2), 177—86.
536. THOMPSON, E.P. (1970). *Warwick University Ltd.* Harmondsworth: Penguin Books.
537. UNIVERSITY OF BIRMINGHAM. (1972). Report of the review body appointed by the University. Birmingham: the University.
538. UNIVERSITY OF CAMBRIDGE. (1967). Report to the Council of the Senate on the administration organization of the University. Cambridge University Press.
539. UNIVERSITY OF EDINBURGH. (1974). Constitution and Structure Committee. (Chairman: Sir William Murie). Report and university report 2 vols. Edinburgh: the University.
540. UNIVERSITY OF OXFORD (1966). Commission of Inquiry (Chairman: Lord Franks) Report: 2 vols. Oxford: Clarendon Press.
541. COMMITTEE OF ENQUIRY INTO THE GOVERNANCE OF THE UNIVERSITY OF LONDON. (1972). (Chairman: Lord Murray of Newhaven) Final Report. University of London.

542. UNIVERSITIES CENTRAL COUNCIL ON ADMIS-
     SIONS. Reports 1961–3+. Thence annually.
     UCCA 1964 onwards. (Cheltenham, UCCA since
     1968).
543. YOUNG, R. (1973). The Roger Young enquiry: report
     on the policies and running of Stirling University
     from 1966–73 made to the University Court.
     Stirling: University of Stirling.
See also 3(h) (iv); 15, 19, 22, 28, 30, 184, 194, 198

6(f) (ii) *Vice Chancellors*
544. COLLISON, P. (1969). 'University heads: who are
     they?', *N. Soc.* 13, 12–14.
545. COLLISON, P. and MILLEN, J. (1969). 'University
     Chancellors, Vice-chancellors and College princi-
     pals: a social profile', *Sociol.* 3, 77–109.
546. DUNDONALD, J. (pseud.) (1962). *Letters to a Vice
     Chancellor*. Edward Arnold.
547. SZRETER, R. (1968). 'An academic patriate – Vice-
     chancellors 1966–7', *Univs. Qu.* 23 (1), 17–45.
See also 3(h) (iv)

6(f) (iii) *administration*
548. AITKEN, (Sir) R. (1966). *Administration of a univer-
     sity*. University of London Press.
549. ANGUS, W.S. (1973). 'University administrative staff',
     Pub. Adm. 51, 17–40.
550. BROOKS, G.E. (1973). 'Administrative modernization
     in British Universities', *Univs. Qu.* 27 (4), 431–56.
551. CHRISTOPHERSON, Sir D. (1973). *The university at
     work*. SCM Press.
552. CHRISTOPHERSON, Sir D. (1968). 'The formulation
     of academic policy', *Ed. f. Teaching* 77, 5–13.
553. FIELDEN, J. and LOCKWOOD, G. (1973). *Planning
     and management in universities*. Chatto and
     Windus.
554. LOCKWOOD, G. (1972). 'University planning and
     management techniques', Paris: O.E.C.D.
555. MILLER, G.W. (1976). 'Staff development pro-
     grammes in British universities and polytechnics,'
     Paris: IIEP.

556. PERKIN, H. (1974). 'Adaptation to change by British universities,' *Univs. Qu.* 28 (4), 389—403.
556A. PIPER, D.W. and GLATTER, R. (1977). *The Changing University: a report on staff development in universities.* Windsor: NFER Publishing Co.
557. SHATTOCK, M. (1970). 'A changing pattern of university administration', *Univs. Qu.* 24 (3), 310—20.
See also 6(f) (vii), 54

6(j) (iv) *planning and finance*
558. ARMITAGE, P. and SMITH, C.S. (1972). 'Controllability: an example', *Higher Ed. Rev.* 5 (1), 55—66.
559. BULLOCK, N., DICKENS, P. and STEADMAN, P. (1968). 'A theoretical model for university planning', *Univs. Qu.* 22 (2), 124—41.
560. CARTER, C.F. (1972). 'The efficiency of universities', *Higher Ed.* 1 (i), 77—89.
561. FERNS, H.S. (1967). 'A radical proposal for the Universities', *Pol. Qu.* 38, 276—82.
562. LAYARD, R. and KING, J. (1968). 'The impact of Robbins', *Higher Ed. Rev.* I (I), 7—26.
563. LAYARD, R. and others. (1969). *The impact of Robbins.* Harmondsworth: Penguin Books.
564. MORRIS, A. (1973). 'The quinquennial settlement: a commentary', *Higher Ed. Rev.* 5 (2), 26—57.
565. MORRIS, A. (1975). 'Separate funding of university teaching and research', *Higher Ed. Rev.* 7 (2), 42—58.
566. MORRIS, A.C. (1972). 'Resourcefulness and the U.G.C.', *Univs. Qu.* 26 (4), 429—39.
567. MORRIS, A.C. and SIMS, M.A. (1972). 'Inflation, supplementation and university productivity' *Higher Ed. Rev.* 5 (1), 33—54.
568. MORRIS, (Sir) C. and others. (1964). 'Second thoughts on Robbins', *Univs. Qu.* 18 (2), 119—68.
569. PERKIN, H. (1972). 'University planning in Britain in the 1960s', *Higher Ed.* 1 (1), 111—20.
570. PICKFORD, M. (1974). 'Costing university resources', *Univs. Qu.* 28 (3), 349—61.

571. PICKFORD, M. (1975). *University expansion and finance.* Brighton: Sussex University Press.
572. ROBBINS, Lord and FORD, B. (1965). 'Report on Robbins', *Univs. Qu.* 20 (1), 5—15.
573. SIMPSON, M.G. and others. (1972). Planning university development. Paris, OECD.

6(j) (v) *Research*
574. FINCH, A.C.M. (1963). 'Financing University Research', *Univs. Qu.* 17 (3), 238—48.
575. PRATT, J. (1972). 'More government in R and D.', *Higher Ed. Rev.* 4 (2), 33—44.
576. SCOTT, P. (1972). 'The universities and the research councils in Britain', *Higher Ed.* 1 (i), 121—6.

6(j) (vi). *Student participation*
577. ASHBY, Sir E. (1970). *Masters and scholars: reflection on the rights and responsibilities of students.* Oxford University Press.
578. ASHBY, Sir E. and ANDERSON, M. (1970). *The rise of the student estate in Britain.* Macmillan.
579. BELL, D.A. *et al.,* (1972). 'A survey of student representation on university senates', *Univs. Qu.* 27 (1), 40—45.
580. BLACKSTONE, T. and others (1970). *Students in conflict LSE.* Weidenfeld.
581. UNIVERSITY OF CAMBRIDGE (Lord Devlin, High Steward) (1973). Report of the sit-in in February 1972 and its consequences. Cambridge University Press.
582. COMMITTEE OF VICE-CHANCELLORS AND PRINCIPALS OF THE UNIVERSITIES OF THE U.K. (1971). Student participation in university government. CVC. 1971.
583. CROUCH, C. (1970). *The student revolt.* Bodley Head.
584. HOCH, P. and SCHOENBACH, V. (1969). *L.S.E. The natives are restless.* Sheed and Ward.
585. KIDD, H. (1969). *The troubles at L.S.E.* Oxford University Press.
586. MARTIN, D.C. (ed.) (1969). *Anarchy and culture.* Routledge and Kegan Paul.

587. UNIVERSITY OF OXFORD (1969). Committee on relations with Junior Members — Report. Oxford University Press.

588. ROOKE, M.A. (1971). *Anarchy and apathy: student unrest 1968–70.* Hamish Hamilton.

589. SEARLE, J.R. (1972). *The campus war.* Harmondsworth: Penguin Books. 1972.

590. STRAW, J. (1977). 'The finance of student unions', *Higher Ed. Rev.*, 4 (2), 45–56.

See also 189

6(j) (vii) *new universities*

591. BELOFF, M. (1968). *The plateglass universities.* Secker and Warburg.

592. DAICHES, D. (ed.) (1964). *The idea of a new university: an experiment in Sussex.* Deutsch.

593. JOBLING, R.G. (1970). 'The location and siting of a new university', *Univs. Qu.* 24 (2). 123–36.

594. LOCKWOOD, G. (1972). 'Planning a university', *Higher Ed.* 1 (4), 409–34.

595. LOWE, R.A. (1969). 'Determinants of a university's curriculum', *Br. J. Ed. Studs.* XVII, 41–53.

596. PERKIN, H.J. (1969). *New universities in the United Kingdom.* Paris, OECD: HMSO.

597. SLOMAN, A.E. (1964). *A university in the making.* British Broadcasting Corporation.

6(j) (viii) *university teachers*

598. HALSEY, A.M. and TROW, M.A. (1971). *The British academics.* Faber.

599. PERKIN, H.J. (1969). *Key profession: the history of university teachers.* Routledge and Kegan Paul.

600. TROW, M. and HALSEY, A.H. (1969). 'British academics and the professorship', *Sociol.* 3, 321–39.

601. WILLIAMS, G. (1973). 'University recruitment 1968/9 and 1970/1', *Univs. Qu.* 27 (2), 172–99.

602. WILLIAMS, G. and others. (1974). *The academic labour market.* Amsterdam: Elsevier Scientific. 1974.

See also 228, 229

6(j) (ix) *miscellaneous*
603. CAINE, Sir S. (1969). *British universities: purpose and prospects.* Bodley Head.
604. COLLISON, P. (1976). 'The university and local politics', *Oxf. Rev. Ed.* 2 (1), 71–84.
605. GOLDMAN, R.J. (1966). 'The changing role of University Departments of Education', *Ed. f. Teaching* 70, 13–21.
606. MOUNTFORD, Sir J. (1966). *British universities.* Oxford University Press.
607. NIBLETT, W.R. (1975). 'The functions and problems of universities today', *Asp. Ed.* 18, 102–116.
608. NIBLETT, W.R. (1974). *Universities between two worlds.* University of London Press.
609. PETERS, R.S. (1972). 'The role and responsibilities of the universities in teacher education', *Lond. Ed. Rev.* 1, 14–23.
610. ROBBINS, Lord (1966). 'Of academic freedom', *Univs. Qu.* 20 (4), 420–35.
See also 102

Social Aspects

7(a) *General*
611. ARMITAGE, P. and CRAMPIN, A. (1971). *Raising the school leaving age, comprehensive reorganization and the demand for higher education.* London School of Economics.
612. BERNSTEIN, B. (1967). 'Open schools, open society?', *N. Soc.* 10 (259), 351–3.
613. DONNISON, D.V. (1967). 'Education and opinion', *N. Soc.* 10 (265), 583–7.
614. HAMPTON, W. (1972). 'Local authorities and the making of social policy', *Pol. Studs.*, XX, 222–25.
615. HILL, D.M. (1970). *Participating in local affairs.* Harmondsworth: Penguin Books.
616. ROBINSON, E.E. (1969). 'Education as a social service', *Pol. Qu.* 40, 56–65.
617. WARNOCK, M. (1976). 'Education and its purposes', *N. Soc.* 38 (737), 353–5.
See also 85, 91

7(b) *Home and School*
618. ACLAND, H. (1971). 'Does parent involvement matter?', *N. Soc.* 18 (468), 507–10.
619. BACON, A.W. (1976). 'Parent power and professional control — a case study in the engineering of client consent', *Sociol. Rev.* 24 (3), 577–97.
620. BURGESS, T. (1976). *Home and school* (revised edition). Harmondsworth: Penguin Books.
612. CAVE, R.G. (1970). *Partnership for change: parents and schools.* Ward Lock Educational.
622. COHEN, L. (1970). 'Problems in home–school cooperation: the headteacher's point of view', *Sociol. Rev.* 18 (3), 393–406.
623. CORBETT, A. (1967). 'One-class schools?', *N. Soc.* 10 (249), 16–18.
624. CRAFT, M. *et. al.*, (1972). *Linking home and school.* Longman.
625. GOODACRE, E. (1972). *School and home.* Slough: National Foundation for Educational Research.
626. GREEN, L. (1968). *Parents and teachers: partners or rivals?* Allen and Unwin.
626. PARTINGTON, J.A. (1970). 'Parents, zoning and the choice of school', *J. Ed. Adm. Hist.* II (2), 39–45.
628. WARRIOR, D. and TUCKWELL, P. (1972). 'Home and school', *N. Soc.* 22 (524). 148–50.
629. YOUNG, M. and McGEENEY, P. (1968). 'Parent power: proposals for parent participation in schools', *N. Soc.* 12 (301).

7(c) *Equality of opportunity*
630. BIRLEY, D. and DUFTON, A. (1971). *An equal chance: equalities and inequalities of educational opportunity.* Routledge and Kegan Paul.
631. BYRNE, D. and others. (1975). *The poverty of education.* Martin Robertson.
632. BYRNE, E. and WILLIAMSON, W. (1972). 'Regional variations in educational provisions — the case of the North-East', *Sociol.* 6 (i), 71–87.
633. BYRNE, E.M. (1975). 'Educational achievement and regional inequality with particular reference to the

North East', *Dur. Res. Rev.* VII (35), 1029–36.

634. CLEGG, A. and MEESON, B. (1973). *Children in distress.* Harmondsworth: Penguin Books.

635. KING, R. (1974). 'Social class, educational attainment and provision: an LEA case study', *Pol. Polt.* 3 (1), 17–36.

636. MEDLICOTT, P. (1974). 'The hidden 11-plus', *N. Soc.* 29 (613), 11–13.

637. TAYLOR, G. (1971). 'North and south: the education split', *N. Soc.* 17 (440), 346–7.

638. TAYLOR, G. and AYRES, N. (1969). *Born and bred unequal.* Longman.

See also 4(k), 5(c), 191, 192

7(d) *Compensatory education*

639. ACLAND, H. (1971). 'What is a bad school?', *N. Soc.* 18 (467), 450–53.

640. CORBETT, A. (1969). 'Are educational priority areas working?', *N. Soc.* 14 (372), 763–7.

641. CORBETT, A. (1968). 'Priority schools', *N. Soc.* 11 (296).

642. DEPARTMENT OF EDUCATION AND SCIENCE. Educational priority

    Vol. I EPA Problems and Policies (ed. Halsey A.H.) HMSO 1972

    Vol. II EPA Surveys and Statistics (ed. Halsey A.H.) HMSO 1974

    Vol. III The West Riding Digest (ed. Smith E.) HMSO 1975

    Vol. IV EPA– A Scottish Study (ed. Morrison A.) Edinburgh HMSO 1974

643. HATCH, S. and SHERROTT, R. (1973). 'Positive discrimination and the distribution of deprivations', *Pol. Polt.* 1 (3), 223–40.

644. RAYNOR, S. and HARDEN, J. (1973). *Equality and city schools* Vols. 1–2. Routledge and Kegan Paul/Oxford University Press.

7(e) *Recurrent education*

645. BUCHANAN, D. and PERCY, K. (1969). *Emergent*

patterns in LEA adult education. National Institute of Adult Education.

646. CANTOR, L.M. (1974). Recurrent education: policy and development in OECD member countries: United Kingdom. Paris, OECD.

647. DEPARTMENT OF EDUCATION AND SCIENCE COMMITTEE OF ENQUIRY INTO THE PROBLEMS AT FIRCROFT COLLEGE. (1976). Report of a Committee ... under the chairmanship of Andrew Leggett. HMSO.

648. HOULT, D.A. (1975). 'The Open University', *Asp. Ed.* 127–44.

649. PRATT, J. (1971). 'Open, University!', *Higher Ed. Rev.* 3 (2), 6–24.

650. OPEN UNIVERSITY (1976). Committee on continuing education: Interim Report. Milton Keynes: Open University.

651. TUNSTALL, J. (ed.) (1974). *The Open University opens.* Routledge and Kegan Paul.

See also 88

7(f) *Community education*

652. CORBETT, A. (1969). 'Community School,' *New Soc.* 13 (335), 313–4.

653. EDUCATION DIGEST. (9.8.74). Community relations. Education Supplement, i–ix.

654. McGEENEY, P. (1972). 'Community involvement and educational change,' *Forum 14* (2), 45–7.

7(g) *Welfare*
(i) *guidance*

655. MOORE, B.M. (1970). *Guidance in comprehensive schools: a study of five systems.* Slough: NFER.

656. WHITE, J. (1970). 'The concept of the school counsellor', *Ed. f. Teaching* 82, 34–41.

657. WILLIAMS, P. (1965). 'The school psychological service', *N. Soc.* 5 (123), 17–18.

(ii) *School meals*

658. CORBETT, A. (1966). 'The school meals question', *N. Soc.* 8 (199).

659. DAVIES, B. and REDDIN, M. (1967). 'School meals and Plowden', *N. Soc.* 9 (241), 690—91.
660. DAVIES, B., REDDIN, M. and DALE, A. (1971). 'Some constraints on school meals policy', *Soc. Econ. Adm.* 5 No. 1, 34—52.

(iii) *other aspects*
661. AYERST, D. (1965). 'Tackling the tough schools', *N. Soc.* 5 (121), 18—19.
662. CORBETT, A. (1966). 'Education maintenance grants', *N. Soc.* (215), 721—22.
663. CORBETT, A. (1971). 'No more kid-catchers', *N. Soc.* 17 (440), 352—53.
664. EDUCATION — Digest (16.2.73). 'Service of youth', *Edn*, i—viii.
665. FITZHERBERT, K. (1973). 'Social work and school', *N. Soc.* 23 (540), 294—5.
666. MEDLICOTT, P. (1973). 'The truancy 'problem',' *N. Soc.* (573), 768—70.
667. PAYNE, P. (1973). 'Aid for a pupil', *N. Soc.* 25 (567), 397—8.
668. ROBERTS, K. (1970). 'The youth employment service, the schools and the preparation of school leavers for employment', *Voc. Asp. Ed.* 22, 81—89.
See also 186

7(h) *Special Education*
669. JACKSON, S. (1969). *Special education in England and Wales.* Oxford University Press.
670. MEDLICOTT, P. (1974). 'Special teaching for special children', *N. Soc.* 27 (598), 698—701.
671. TIZARD, J. (1975). 'The objectives and organizations of educational and day care services for young children,' *Oxf. Rev. Ed.* 1 (3), 211—22.
672. YOUNGHUSBAND (Dame) E. (ed.) (1970). *Living with handicap*: Report of a working party on children with special needs. National Bureau for Co-operation in Child Care.

Curriculum Control

8(a) *Curriculum development*

673. BANKS, L.J. (1969). 'Curriculum developments in Britain 1963–8', *J. Curr. Studs.* 1 (3), 247–59.

674. BASSETT, G.W. (1970). *Innovation in primary education*. Wiley.

675. COLLIER, K.G. (1972). 'Innovation: Criteria of judgement', *Br. J. Ed. Technol.* 3 (3), 175–85.

676. CORBETT, A. (1968). 'Reforming the school curriculum', *N. Soc.* 11 (270), 118–122.

677. DALIN, P. (1970). The management of innovation in education. Paris, O.E.C.D.

678. DAVIES, I.K. (1971). *The management of learning*. McGraw Hill.

678A DEVLIN, T. and WARNOCK, M. (1977). *What must we teach?* Temple Smith.

678B GLATTER, R. (ed.) (1977). *Control of the curriculum: issues and trends in Britain and Europe*. University of London Institute of Education.

679. HARRIS, A. and others (eds.) (1975). *Curriculum innovation*. Croom Helm.

680. HOOPER, R. (ed.) (1971). *The curriculum: context design and development*. Oliver and Boyd.

681. HOYLE, E. (1969). 'How does the curriculum change?', *J. Curr. Studs.*
I – A proposal for inquiries 1 (2) May 1969 132–41.
II – systems and strategies 1 (3) Nov. 1969 230–39.

682. HOYLE, E. (1970). 'Planned organizational change in education,' *Res. Ed.* 3, 1–22.

683. IRVINE SMITH, R. (1966). 'Curricular reform', *N. Soc.* 189, 12–15.

684. JUDGE, H.G. (1976). 'The great curriculum row', *N. Soc.* 733, 119–20.

685. KERR, J.F. (1968). *Changing the curriculum*. University of London Press.

686. OWEN, J.G. (1969). 'Strategies of curriculum innovation,' *J. Curr. Studs*, 1 (1), 19–25.

687. OWEN, J.G. (1973). *The management of curriculum development*. Cambridge University Press.
688. OWEN, J. (1970). 'Educational Innovation: the human factor', *J. Ed. Adm. Hist.* II–2, 46–53.
689. REID, W.A. and WALKER, D.F. (eds.) (1975). *Case studies in curriculum change: Great Britain and the United States*. Routledge.
689A SECRETARY OF STATE FOR EDUCATION AND SCIENCE SECRETARY OF STATE FOR WALES. (1977). *Education in Schools*: a consultative document. HMSO.
690. SHAW, K.E. (1972). 'Curriculum Decision-making in a college of education', *J. Curr. Studs.*, 4 (1), 51–9.
691. SHIPMAN, M.D. *et. al.*, (1974). *Inside a curriculum project*. Methuen.
692. SMITH, M.P. (1971). 'Curriculum change at the local level,' *J. Curr. Studs.* 3 (2), 158–62.
693. STENHOUSE, L. (1975). *An introduction to curriculum research and development*. Heinemann.
694. WALTON, J. (1972). 'The implications of innovation', *Forum* 14 (2), 38–42.
See also 55, 89, 98, 101, 238

8(b) *Examinations*
695. BRUCE, G. (1969). *School examinations*. Oxford: Pergamon Press.
696. JUDGE, H.G. (1974). 'Exams and school-leavers: chaos and change', *N. Soc.* 26 (614), 77–79.
697. MACINTOSH, H.G. (1970). 'A constructive role for examining boards in curriculum development', *J. Curr. Studs.* 2 (1), 32–39.
698. MACINTOSH, H.G. (1969). 'The organization of the Associated Examining Board', *J. Ed. Adm. Hist.* II (1), 36–41.
699. MONTGOMERY, R.J. (1965). *School examinations: an account of their evolution as administrative devices*. Longman.
700. PEARCE, J. (1972). *School examinations*. Collier–Macmillan.

701. STANDING CONFERENCE OF REGIONAL EXAMINATIONS BOARDS FOR THE CERTIFICATE OF SECONDARY EDUCATION. (1974). An administrative structure for secondary school examinations. The conference (Sheffield).
702. WARNOCK, M. (1976). 'A 16-plus disaster', *N. Soc.* 35 (700), 547–8.

8(c) *Educational Technology*
703. BLACK, J. (1970). 'British Universities since the Brynmor Jones Report', *Br. J. Ed. Technol.* 1 (1).
704. BRIAULT, E.W.H. (1973). 'Resources for learning', *Ed. Adm. (Bull).* 2 (1), 1–10.
705. BRIAULT, E. (1970). 'Educational technology in Inner London Schools and Colleges', *Br. J. Ed. Technol.* 1 (2), 95–106.
706. HARRIS, D. (1976). 'Educational technology at the Open University: a short history of achievement and cancellations', *Br. J. Ed. Technol.* 7 (3), 43–53.
707. HAVELOCK, R.E. (1971). 'The utilisation of educational research and development', *Br. J. Ed. Technol.* 2 (2). 1971.
708. HAWKRIDGE, D.F. (1976). 'Next year, Jerusalem! the rise of educational technology', *Br. J. Ed. Technol.* 7 (1), 7–30.
709. HUBBARD, G. (1976). 'Issues and public policies in educational technology', *Br. J. Ed. Technol.* 7 (3), 51–8.
710. HUBBARD, G. (1972). 'James and educational technology,' *Br. J. Ed. Technol.* 3 (2), 102–7.
711. JONES, H.C. (1972). 'The management of teaching management functions in teaching', *Br. J. Ed. Technol.* 3 (3), 199–214.
712. LEWIS, B.N. (1971). 'Course production at the Open University,' *Br. J. Ed. Technol.*
    I – Some basic problems
        2(1) Jan 1971 4–13
    II – Activities and activity networks
        2(2) May 1971 111–23

III Planning and scheduling
3(3) Oct 1971 189–205
2(2) May 1971 108–28

713. LEWIS, B.N. (1973). 'Educational technology at the Open University: an approach to the problem of quality', *Br. J. Ed. Technol.* 4 (3), 188–203.

714. MACKENZIE, N. and others. (1970). 'Audio-visual resources in Sussex schools', *Br. J. Ed. Technol.* 1 (1), 16–34.

715. MACKENZIE, N. (1966). 'Education and the new technology', *Tech. Ed.* 8, 540–4.

716. RICHMOND, W.K. (1969). *The education industry.* Methuen.

717. TAYLOR, G. (1969). 'Educating the 'Edmass', a technology of learning', *N. Soc.* 13 (351), 947–9.

See also 500

The teaching profession

9(a) *Professionalism*

718. BOOTH, I.G. (1973). 'Some political features of the Teaching Council movement', *Dur. Res. Rev.* VI (30). 725–34.

719. DEEM, R. (1976). 'Professionalism, unity and militant action: the case of teachers', *Sociol. Rev.* 24 (1), 43–62.

720. GOSDEN, P.H.J.H. (1972). *The evolution of a profession.* Oxford: Blackwell.

721. HOYLE, E. (74). 'Professionality, professionalism and control in teaching', *Lond. Ed. Rev.* 3 (2), 14–19.

722. KELSALL, R.K. and H.M. (1969). *The school teacher in England and the United States.* Oxford: Pergamon.

723. LEGGATT, T. (1970). *Teaching as a profession* (in Professions and professionalization, ed. JACKSON, J.A.) Cambridge University Press.

724. PURVIS, J. (1973). 'School teaching as a professional career,' *Br. J. Sociol* XXIV (1), 43–57.

725. TAYLOR, W. (ed.) (Summer 1974). 'Teaching as a profession', *Lond. Ed. Rev.* 3 2.
See also 92

9(b) *Teacher education policy*

726. BOYLE (Lord) and others. (1972). 'Report on James', *Univs. Qu.* 26 (2), 127–63.
727. CORTIS, G.A. (1972). 'The James Report: attitudes of senior staffs in the colleges', *Higher Ed. Rev.* 4 (3), 3–12.
728. FORD, B. (1974). 'The emancipation of teacher training', *Univs. Qu.* 29 (1), 7–43.
729. CROUCH, C. *et al.*, (1973). 'Framework for binary consummation', *Univs. Qu.* 27 (2), 133–56.
730. LEWIS, I. (1966). 'Problems facing the teaching profession', *Planning*, 32 498. *Political and Economic Planning*.
731. McCONNELL, T.R. and FRY, M.A. (1972). 'Flexibility or rigidity: university attitudes towards the James Report', *Higher Ed. Rev.* Vol. 4 (3), 13–29.
732. MEDLICOTT, P. (1974). 'Teacher training in flux', *N. Soc.* 30 (626), 15–17.
733. NIBLETT, W.R. (1972). 'The place of teacher education in the structure of higher education', *Lond. Ed. Rev.* I (1), 6–13.
734. NIBLETT, W.R. and others. (1975). *The university connection*. Windsor, NFER Publishing Co.
735. PARRY, J.P. (1972). *The Lord James tricycle*. Allen and Unwin.
736. TAYLOR, W. (ed.) (1969). *Towards a policy for the education of teachers*. Butterworths.
See also 6(e) (i) 93, 127, 190, 208

9(c) *In-service education*

737. CAVE, R.E. (1974). 'In-service education after the White Paper — an LEA Inspector's viewpoint', *Camb. J. Ed.* 4 (2), 52–59.
738. ERAUT, M. (1972). *In-service education for innovation*. National Council for Educational Technology.

739. THOMPSON, E.M. (1972). 'Teachers' Centres: why they were established by LEAS instead of Institutes of Education', *Dur. Res. Rev.* VI (291), 678–89.
740. THORNBURY, R. (1974). 'Teachers' Centres', *N. Soc.* 28 (612). 761–3.
741. WATKINS, R. (ed.) (1973). *In-service training: structure and content.* Ward Lock.

9(d) *Recruitment and supply*
742. AHAMAD, B. (1970). 'A post mortem on teacher supply forecasts', *Higher Ed. Rev.* 2 (3), 41–7.
743. DEPARTMENT OF EDUCATION AND SCIENCE NATIONAL ADVISORY COUNCIL ON THE TRAINING AND SUPPLY OF TEACHERS. (1965). 9th Report. The demand for and supply of teachers. HMSO.
744. KELSALL, R.K. (1963). *Women and teaching.* HMSO.
745. OLLERENSHAW, Dame K. (1974). *Returning to teaching.* Councils and Education Press.
746. PARTINGTON, G. (1976). *Women teachers in the twentieth century in England and Wales.* Windsor: NFER Publishing Co.
See also 97, 100

9(e) *Teacher Associations*
747. BLUM, A.A. (ed.) (1969). *Teacher unions and associations: a comparative study.* Urbana London University of Illinois Press.
748. COATES, D. (1972). 'The Teachers Associations and the restructuring of Burnham', *Br. J. Ed. Studs.* XX, 192–204.
749. COATES, R.D. (1972). *Teacher unions and interest group politics.* Cambridge University Press.
750. CORBETT, A. (1966). 'The anti-feminists?', *N. Soc.* 8 (201) 193.
751. EDUCATION – Digest (15.6.73). 'Teachers' Unions', *Edn,* i–viii.
752. FARNHAM, D. (1975). 'How apt is APT? (The Association of Polytechnic Teachers)', *Higher Ed. Rev.* 7 (3), 39–52.

753. FEARN, E. and BALL, C. (1972). 'Teacher participation and the G.C.E. Boards: the role of the NUT Standing Committees', *J. Ed. Adm. Hist.* IV (2), 39–46.
754. GRETTON, J. and CRANE, A. (1975). *Teachers in the British general election of October 1974.* Times Newspapers.
755. GRIFFITHS, T. (1970). *The teacher's strike (1969–70).* National Union of Teachers.
756. MANZER, R.A. (1970). *Teachers and politics*: the role of the National Union of Teachers in the making of national education policy in England and Wales since 1944. Manchester: Manchester U.P.
757. MEDLICOTT, P. (1974). 'What the NUT does', *N. Soc.* 30 (637), 754–5.
758. MORTON, B. (1969). *Action 1919–69* (a record of the growth of the National Association of Schoolmasters) Hemel Hempstead: NAS.
759. ROY, W. (1968). *The teachers' union.* Schoolmaster Press.
760. TIPTON, B.F.A. (1975). 'The hidden side of teaching: the teachers' unions', *Lond. Ed. Rev.* 3 (2), 20–30.

9(f) *Miscellaneous*
761. BURKE, V. (1971). *Teachers in turmoil.* Harmondsworth: Penguin Books.
762. HILSUM, S. and START, K.B. (1974). *Promotion and careers in teaching.* Windsor: NFER Publishing Co.
763. SILVER, H. (1976). 'Teaching: the death of a meal ticket', *N. Soc.* 37 (728), 592–4.
764. TURNER, J.D. and RUSHTON, J. (ed.) (1974). *The teacher in a changing society.* Manchester: Manchester University Press.

Scotland, Wales and N. Ireland

Scotland

10(a) (i) *Scottish Education Department Annual Reports*
765. SCOTTISH EDUCATION DEPARTMENT: EDUCATION IN SCOTLAND. (Various Dates). A report of the Secretary of State for Scotland (Annually). Edinburgh: HMSO.
766. SCOTTISH EDUCATION DEPARTMENT CONSULTATIVE COMMITTEE ON THE CURRICULUM (Various dates). Reports. Edinburgh: HMSO.

10(a) (ii) *S.E.D. papers on teacher recruitment and supply*
767. SCOTTISH EDUCATION DEPARTMENT. (1963). Committee on the arrangements for the award and withdrawal of Certificates of Competency to teach. Edinburgh: HMSO.
768. SCOTTISH EDUCATION DEPARTMENT. (1963). Departmental Committee on numbers of teachers required for service in Scotland. Edinburgh: HMSO.

(10)(a) (iii) *Other S.E.D. papers*
769. SCOTTISH EDUCATION DEPARTMENT. (1969). Review of the constitution and functions of the General Teaching Council: memorandum by the Secretary of State for Scotland. Edinburgh: HMSO.
770. SCOTTISH EDUCATION DEPARTMENT. (1966–1967). Teacher education training and certification: Memorandum on entry requirements and courses. Edinburgh: HMSO.
771. SCOTTISH EDUCATION DEPARTMENT COMMITTEE OF INQUIRY INTO ADULT EDUCATION IN SCOTLAND. (1975). Adult education: The challenge of change. Report by a committee of inquiry appointed by the Secretary of State for Scotland under the chairmanship of K.J.W. Alexander. Edinburgh: HMSO.

772. SCOTTISH EDUCATION DEPARTMENT. (1962). Consultation on educational matters: report of the working party on consultation between the teachers' associations and the S.E.D. on educational matters. Edinburgh: HMSO.
773. SCOTTISH EDUCATION DEPARTMENT. (Various Dates). Education in (various Scottish counties). Reports by H.M. Inspector of Schools. Edinburgh: HMSO.
774. SCOTTISH EDUCATION DEPARTMENT. (1976). The raising of the school-leaving age in Scotland: a report by H.M. Inspectors of Schools. Edinburgh: HMSO.
775. SCOTTISH EDUCATION DEPARTMENT. (1973). Secondary school staffing: a report on secondary school organization and staffing in Scotland, with proposals for new staffing standards. Edinburgh: HMSO.

10(a) (iv) *other Government papers*
776. COMMISSION FOR LOCAL GOVERNMENT IN SCOTLAND. (1975—76). Annual Reports 1975 +; Edinburgh, The Commission.
777. ROYAL COMMISSION ON LOCAL GOVERNMENT IN SCOTLAND. (1969). (Chairman — Lord Wheatley) Report and appendices. Edinburgh HMSO.

10(a) (v) *other publications*
778. BONE, T.R. (1967). 'The changing pattern of school inspection in Scotland', *Scot. Ed. Studs.* 1 (1), 46—51.
779. BONE, T.R. (1974). 'The General Teaching Council for Scotland: its achievements', *Lond. Ed. Rev.* 3 (2), 51—59.
780. CUMMING, C.E. (1968). 'Patterns of expenditure in Scottish education authorities', *Scot. Ed. Studs.* 1 (2), 61—67.
781. CURRAN, S.C. (1968). 'Educational technology', *Scot. Ed. Studs.* 1 (2), 3—8.
782. DELL, E.A. (1969). 'Thirty years of child guidance;

the development of the Glasgow child guidance service', *Scot. Ed. Studs.* 1 (3), 32–40.

783. FINDLAY, I.R. (1973). *Education in Scotland.* Newton Abbot: David and Charles.

784. GATHERER, W.A. (1976). 'Curriculum development in a regional context', *Scot. Ed. Studs.* 8 (2), 84–94.

785. GRAHAM, N.W. (1965). 'The administration of education in Scotland', *Pub. Adm.* 43, 299–312.

786. HUNTER, S.L. (1972). *The Scottish educational system* (2nd edn.) Oxford: Pergamon.

787. MACBETH, A. and MACKENZIE, M. (1976). 'Community participation and the Scottish school councils', *Scot. Ed. Studs.* 8 (2), 106–112.

788. McLELLAN, A. (1976). 'Education since reorganization', *Scot. Ed. Studs.* 8 (2), 75–83.

789. MORRIS, J.G. (1976). Innovation and development in the Scottish educational system', *Scot. Educ. Studs.* 8 (2), 67–74.

790. SMITH, I. (1974). 'Educational decision-making – a case study', *Scot. Ed. Studs.* 6 (2), 77–85.

10(b) *Wales*

791. COMMISSION FOR LOCAL ADMINISTRATION IN WALES. (1975–6). Annual Reports 1975, 76 Cardiff, the Commission.

792. JENKINS, T.R. (1975). 'Teacher training in Welsh Colleges of Education 1960–70'. *J. Ed. Adm. Hist.* VII (2), 31–39.

793. MADGWICK, P.J. (1970). 'The Welsh Joint Education Committee – a political analysis', *J. Ed. Adm. Hist.* III (1), 38–49.

794. WELSH EDUCATION OFFICE. (1975). Small primary schools in Wales. Cardiff: The Office.

795. WILLIAMS, L.H. (1971). 'The changing pattern of secondary education in Montgomeryshire since 1945', *J. Ed. Adm. Hist.* III, 25–41.

See also 87

10(c) *Northern Ireland*

796. NORTHERN IRELAND — MINISTRY OF EDU-
     CATION. (Various dates). Education in Northern
     Ireland (Annually). Belfast: HMSO.

797. ADULT EDUCATION IN NORTHERN IRELAND.
     (1965). Report of the committee appointed by the
     Minister of Education in March 1963. Belfast:
     HMSO.

798. NORTHERN IRELAND MINISTRY OF EDU-
     CATION. (1973). Committee on Teacher Edu-
     cation in Northern Ireland: report of committee of
     enquiry appointed by the Minister of Education
     under the chairmanship of Professor F.J. Lelievre.
     Belfast: HMSO.

799. NORTHERN IRELAND Ministry of Finance. (1965).
     Higher education in Northern Ireland: report of
     the committee appointed by the Minister of
     Finance. Belfast: HMSO.

800. ADVISORY COUNCIL FOR EDUCATION IN NOR-
     THERN IRELAND. (1973). Reorganization of
     secondary education in Northern Ireland. Belfast:
     HMSO.

Information

11(a) (i) *Statistics*
   1. official sources
801. DEPARTMENT OF EDUCATION AND SCIENCE:
     EDUCATION STATISTICS for the United King-
     dom, annually, various dates.
802. STATISTICS OF EDUCATION, special series.
   1. Survey of the curriculum and deployment of teachers
      (secondary schools) 1965—6 Pt. I: teachers HMSO
      1968.
   2. Survey of in-service training for teachers, 1967 HMSO
      1970.
   3. Survey of earnings of qualified manpower in England
      and Wales, 1966—67 HMSO 1971.
   4. Survey of the curriculum and deployment of teachers
      (secondary schools) 1965—66 Pt. II: the curriculum
      HMSO 1971.

803. MINISTRY OF EDUCATION (to 1963) AND DE-PARTMENT OF EDUCATION AND SCIENCE (from 1964). Statistics of Education. HMSO. Annually (several vols.).

804. MINISTRY OF EDUCATION AND DEPARTMENT OF EDUCATION AND SCIENCE. (1963 and 1965). Secondary education in each local education authority area. HMSO.

805. MINISTRY OF EDUCATION AND DEPARTMENT OF EDUCATION AND SCIENCE. (1962 and 1964). SELECTED STATISTICS relating to local Education Authorities in England and Wales. HMSO.

11(a) (ii) *Other Material*

806. Institute of Municipal Treasurers and Accountants Society of County Treasurers. 1966–7. EDUCATION STATISTICS. London and Hertford: The Institute. Annually 1968+.

807. WILLIAMS, K. (ed.) (1974). Education Statistics University of Birmingham (Institute of Local Government Studies). Birmingham.

808. HUDSON, K. (ed.) (1975). Education Statistics Vol. 2. University of Birmingham (Institute of Local Government Studies) Birmingham.

11(b) Bibliographies

809. BARON. G. (1965). *A bibliographical guide to the English Educational system (3rd edn.)*. University of London Athlone Press.

810. BLACKSTONE, T. (1975). *Social policy and administration in Britain: a bibliography*. Frances Pinter.

811. BUNTAN, W.J. (1971). *Comprehensive education: a select annotated bibliography*. Slough: National Foundation for Educational Research.

812. COULSON, A.A. (1975). *School administration and management: a selected annotated bibliograpphy*. Hull: Flag Publications.

812A CRAIGIE, J. (1974). *A bibliography of Scottish Education 1872–1970*. London University Press.

813. GOSDEN, P.H.J.H. (1967). *Educational administration in England and Wales, a bibliographical guide.* Leeds: University of Leeds Institute of Education.

814. HARMAN, G.S. (1974). *The politics of education: a bibliographical guide.* St. Lucia: University of Queensland Press.

815. HEYWOOD, J. (1971). *Bibliography of British technological education and training.* Hutchinson Educational.

816. LAWRENCE, D.M. (1975). *Writings on comprehensive education* – Campaign for comprehensive education.

817. MONKS, T.G. (1968). *A classified list of references on comprehensive education.* Slough: National Foundation for Educational Research.

818. PARRY, T. (1974). *A select bibliography of adult education.* National Institute of Adult Edn.

819. RICHARDS, M.S. (1971). *Comprehensive Bibliography.* Headmasters' Associations Review LXIX (210).

820. SHARROCK, A. (1971). *Home and school: a select annotated bibliography.* Slough: National Foundation for Educational Research.

11(c) *Register and guides to sources*

821. ASLIB. *Index to theses* accepted for higher degrees by the Universities of Great Britain and Ireland, and the Council for National Academic Awards. Aslib, various days, biennially to 1973. Annually from 1974.

822. FOSKETT, D.J. (1965). *How to find out: educational research.* Oxford: Pergamon Press.

823. FOSKETT, D.J. (1977). *The literature and sources of education* in ROBERTS, N. (Ed.) Use of social sciences literature. Butterworths.

824. HUMBY, M. (1975). *A guide to the literature of education.* (3rd edn.) University of London Institute of Education Library.

825. NATIONAL FOUNDATION FOR EDUCATIONAL RESEARCH. (1976). *Register of educational*

research in the United Kingdom 1973–6. Windsor: NFER Publishing Co.

826. VAUGHAN, J.E. and ARGLES, M. (1969). *British government publications concerning education: an introductory guide.* (3rd edn). Liverpool: University of Liverpool School of Education.

11(d) *Newspapers and Periodicals*

In addition to the journals used in the compilation of this bibliography, the following contain from time to time articles relating to some aspect or other of educational administration.

Adult Education
Comprehensive Education
Education
Education and Training (formerly Technical Education)
Local Government Chronicle
Public Finance and Accountancy
Secondary Education
Times Educational Supplement
Times Educational Supplement (Scotland)
Times Higher Education Supplement
Trends in Education
Where?

11(e) *Other material*

Many of the organizations referred to above issue annual reports with varying degrees of detail. These would have been far too numerous to list here, and are therefore excluded: the only exceptions being the Department of Education and Science and the corresponding departments in Scotland and N. Ireland, and the Parliamentary Commissioner for Administration and his equivalents, the Commissioners for Local (including Welsh) Administration. Two accessible and comprehensive sources of information on educational organizations are:

827. THE EDUCATION AUTHORITIES DIRECTORY AND ANNUAL. Redhill: the School Government

Publishing Company, Annually.

828. EDUCATION COMMITTEES YEAR BOOK. Councils and Education Press, Annually.

APPENDIX

Periodicals cited

The following periodicals were used in the preparation of this Bibliography. Except when otherwise stated, the place of publication is London; the abbreviations are in accordance with the British Standards Institution recommendations for the abbreviations of titles of periodicals (1967).

1.	Aspects of Education (Hull)	*Asp. Ed.*
2.	British Journal of Educational Studies	*Br. J. Ed. Studs.*
3.	British Journal of Educational Technology (Newcastle upon Tyne)	*Br. J. Ed. Technol.*
4.	British Journal of Political Science	*Br. J. Pol. Sci.*
5.	British Journal of Sociology	*Br. J. Sociol.*
6.	Cambridge Journal of Education (Cambridge)	*Camb. J. Ed.*
7.	Durham Research Review (Durham)	*Dur. Res. Rev.*
8.	Education	*Edn.*
9.	Education for Teaching	*Ed. f. Teaching*
10.	Educational Administration (Bulletin) (Blagdon)	*Ed. Adm. (Bull).*
11.	Educational Research (Slough)	*Ed. Res.*
12.	Educational Review (Birmingham)	*Ed. Rev.*
13.	Educational Studies (Oxford)	*Ed. Studs.*
14.	Forum (Leicester)	*Forum*
15.	Higher Education	*Higher Ed.*
16.	Higher Education Review (Croydon)	*Higher. Ed. Rev.*
17.	Journal of Curriculum Studies	*J. Curr. Studs.*
18.	Journal of Educational Administration and History (Leeds)	*J. Ed. Adm. Hist.*
19.	Journal of Moral Education (Windsor)	*J. Moral. Ed.*
20.	Journal of Social Policy	*J. Soc. Pol.*
21.	Local Government Studies (Birmingham)	*Loc. Govt. Studs.*
22.	London Educational Review	*Lond. Ed. Rev.*
23	London Review of Public Administration	*Lond. Rev. Pub. Adm.*
24.	Minerva	*Min.*
25.	New Society	*N. Soc.*
26.	Oxford Review of Education (Oxford)	*Oxf. Rev. Ed.*
27.	Parliamentary Affairs	*Parl. Aff.*
28.	Policy and Politics (Canterbury)	*Pol. Polt.*
29	Political Quarterly	*Pol. Qu*
30.	Political Studies	*Pol. Studs.*
31.	Public Administration	*Pub. Adm.*
32.	Research in Education (Manchester)	*Res. Ed.*
33.	Researches and Studies (Leeds)	*Res. Studs.*
34.	Scottish Educational Studies (Edinburgh)	*Scot. Ed. Studs.*
35.	Social and Economic Administration (Easter)	*Soc. Econ. Adm.*
36.	Sociological Review (Keele)	*Sociol. Rev.*
37.	Sociology (Oxford)	*Sociol.*

38.	South West Review of Public Administration (Exeter)	*S.W. Rev. Pub. Adm.*
39.	Technical Education	*Tech. Ed.*
40.	Technical Journal	*Tech. J.*
41.	(New) Universities Quarterly	*(New) Univs. Qu.*
42.	Vocational Aspect of Education	*Voc. Asp. Ed.*